UNFORGETTABLE WALKS

UNFORGETTABLE
WALKS

Julia Bradbury

Quercus

First published in Great Britain in 2016 by

Quercus Editions Ltd
Carmelite House
50 Victoria Embankment
London EC4Y 0DZ

An Hachette UK company

A CIP catalogue record for this book is available
from the British Library

HB ISBN 978 1 78429 884 5
EBOOK ISBN 978 1 78429 883 8

Illustrations and maps © Nicola Budd, Howell Illustration
Pictures © Julia Bradbury

The poems and blog posts on pages 207, 231, 235 and 241 are reproduced
by kind permission of their authors – Mark Proctor, Michael Bradbury,
Ian McMillan and Lynne Rowbottom.

The tweets on pages 123–4 are reproduced by kind permission of their authors.

10 9 8 7 6 5 4 3 2 1

Typeset by CC Book Production

Printed and bound in Great Britain by Clays Ltd, St Ives Plc

I don't have a cat, so this book is for my children.

Thank you to my loves, family, friends, colleagues, advisors, agents and confidantes who make it possible for me to be me. I am very lucky to have people in my life who help me get through every day and allow me to pursue my dreams and passions. And to be a bit of a twat sometimes. You know who you are. I love you.

CONTENTS

Introduction

BRIEF ENCOUNTERS OF A COUNTRYSIDE KIND

*B*est *Walks With A View* – a new TV series of beautiful, bracing walks all across the country, fit for all the family. An enticing offer for any broadcaster, surely? Well, this one anyway. As the legendary Mae West once said, 'I generally avoid temptation, unless I can resist it.' And this – it's a no-brainer.

I've done a lot of things on the telly – from laying hedges with Prince Charles to having the late, great Robin Williams nibble at my stilettos (yep) – and I've spent a considerable amount of my telly life climbing mountains, romping across weather-beaten fields, chatting up shepherds and even burying cow shit (while investigating biodynamic farming), but out of everything, *Wainwright Walks,* a series commissioned with possibly the smallest of expectations, is the thing that has probably had the greatest long-term impact on my life and career.

Filmed for the BBC, the series was a particular highlight for me because: a) I love hiking and have done ever since my dad used to lead me out like a puppy; and b) it was completely different to anything I'd filmed before. I had developed a niche in consumer and factual programme-making and when we starting talking about the *Wainwright* series, I was presenting *Watchdog* on BBC1, alongside Nicky Campbell. The walks were a complete antidote to that kind of programme and they were a 'break-out success', which basically means they were low budget, didn't have marketing back-up – but lots of people watched them anyway.

If you don't know who he is, Alfred Wainwright (who also features in this book prominently) is a walking hero who fell in love with the Lake District and wrote lovingly about it in the 1950s and 1960s. His pictorial guides have become somewhat biblical for outdoor types. I'm probably his complete opposite, but following in his footsteps is a recipe that seemed to work. So, after that, we made more walking programmes – and not just Wainwrights.

I've now hiked across swathes of the Great British Countryside and been as far as South Africa, Germany and Iceland. Canals, railways, rivers – I've hiked a fair few, but it's actually been about eight years since that original series (a lifetime in telly), which is why I'm so excited to be back out here, this time doing my own unforgettable walks with unforgettable views. And, perhaps more importantly, there's always a good pub along the way for that important 'pie-and-pint' moment at the end of a hard slog.

Throughout my life, walking has been important to me. Although I now live in London, I spent my childhood in Sheffield and Rutland, so grew up living and breathing rugged green valleys and undulating hills. But my real passion for the countryside comes from my dad, Michael, who was born in the Peak District and, nearly 75 years later, is still a great devotee. Our walks together, which were usually just the two of us, began my lifelong love affair with walking and inspiring land-scapes. My mum, Chrissi, couldn't be described as the outdoor type herself – her Greek ancestry has created an aversion to cold wet environments – and, perhaps oddly, even though I love stomping around hills and fields, I've inherited that from her. But Mum would provide iron rations and logistical support by meeting us at an agreed venue – usually a pub for Dad's benefit.

What I vividly remember from those childhood days with my dad is the huge satisfaction of reaching the end of a walk, often tired, wet and muddy, but certainly very content and also that feeling of great euphoria directly linked to the great outdoors. And, once you've experienced that, it's hard to let go. At heart, I guess, I'm a country girl and will always have an abiding passion and appreciation for our countryside and green spaces. That's something that I'm keen to pass on and this book, with its eight great walks, allows me to do just that.

I've chosen these particular walks because they represent the diversity of our countryside – from the pretty and picturesque (the Cotswolds and the South Downs), through to the rugged and wild (Cumbria and Edale). Inevitably, people will feel some places have been overlooked and, of course, they have. It's simply impossible to include every place and every type of landscape, so Scotland, Ireland and all those other corners, please forgive me. I can only say 'next time'!

I chose Derbyshire because that is where walking began for me, with my dad, and my heart will always skip a beat when I set foot in The Peaks. It's also at the root of our story as a walking nation: the mass trespass on Kinder Scout ignited our right to roam and cemented our passion for the countryside. The Jurassic Coast is such an iconic landscape, and a great place still to fossil hunt. It's also the only place in the world where 185 million years of the earth's history are sequentially exposed in the geology of the dramatic cliffs – and those are years too good to be ignored. And really, what would a selection of walks be without a visit to the Lake District? Castle Crag may not be an obvious choice, but when you feel it's magic you'll understand why this diminutive fell deserves its own story.

Best Walks With A View has been a very different experience for me because I put on the hiking boots as a mother of three, something I still can't quite believe. After my little boy,

Zephyr, was born four years ago, I had this deep longing to give him a brother or a sister – pretty much as strong as the urge to become a mother in the first place. I was 40 when I gave birth to Zeph and Number Two proved to be a bit more difficult to achieve. However, after a tricky ascent and a few stumbles along the way, I am now the proud mama of *twins*, two girls, Zena and Xanthe. I have often been curious about families heading up into the hills with a horde of kids in tow, especially as soon I'm going to be one of those parents. And the magnificent walks featured in this book are suitable for families and are less than 16km (10 miles) in length. Some have particularly personal resonance, as I walked them with my dad when I was a child, and now I look forward to walking them with my own children, probably with dad in tow.

The book that follows is based on a series that I filmed for ITV and I have a television crew in tow. People often ask me about the business of being filmed while I'm walking and remark that it must be hard work for the camera crew to walk and film me at the same time. Of course it is. As the well-known quote about Ginger Rogers dancing with Fred Astaire goes: 'She did everything that he did but backwards in high heels.' It's the same for Jan, my cameraman, minus the heels. Add rough gritty tracks and precipitous cliffs into the mix and things get really interesting.

So the crew are with me every step of the way. Without them pulling together we couldn't get the programmes made (or drink as much tea). Eric, the executive producer of the series that goes with this book, is a warm, lively Liverpudlian who, in his own words, has a mouth 'as big as the Mersey tunnel'. Eric's also a keen walker and a proud father to three lovely girls. We've worked together on all my walking shows, including the original *Wainwright Walks* series, which he created, so I'll be mentioning him, along with Jan, Colin, the soundman, Josh, the series editor, Holly, my photographer and online content producer, Alex and Fran, producer and researcher and my beloved sister, Gina, who pulls all the information together, as well as pulling me together at the beginning and end of each walk.

From the start, I wanted this book to be more than a walking guide or travelogue; yes there are eight cracking walks on the pages, but this is also an opportunity to rediscover the kind of people who love our green and precious land and live in it. In the following pages, we're going to meet some fascinating characters and inspirational and extraordinary people, such as: adventuring legend Sir Chris Bonington, now in his eighties, who has climbed some of the world's biggest and most terrifying mountains, but loves a little pip of a mountain as much as any; Robin, a wood-crafting genius who has single-handedly revived the art of creating wooden bowls by hand globally; the Rudds, who have a fourth-generation family business making handsome rakes by hand; and Annabelle, a tax accountant-turned-blacksmith, who is continuing on a tradition long associated with men. There are artists, authors, shepherdesses and fell runners, too . . . all people who keep the countryside alive and who have their own particular stories to tell.

In the end, the countryside is a great leveller. Meeting people 'out here' you have no idea who or what lurks beneath the layers. We all wear the same dodgy fleece, anoraks, walking trousers (although I've opted for some on-trend leggings this year), so you really can't tell the bankers from the bakers, the rich from the poor. The countryside is like a huge outdoor church welcoming us all – from city traders attempting to break out of the green mile for the green valleys, to the families camping with their kids for the weekend and the thousands of good-hearted people who walk great lengths for charity every year. So, come on everybody! Let's rejoice in the greenery, celebrate the beauty of our land and nature and delight in that glorious fresh air. If God is a DJ, in the words of Faithless, then *this* is his huge super club. So, come join it and see what it's all about on these beautiful, extraordinary, unforgettable walks.

I

DORSET: THE GOLDEN CAP WALK

'I'm a dinosaur, hear me roar'

My first walk for this brand new series takes me back in time. The last time I was on the Jurassic coast, it was off the scale windy and I was filming for BBC's *Countryfile* series with well-known local fossil hunter and geologist Paddy Howe. As we combed the beach, Paddy shouted at me, 'Keep your head down and your eyes peeled. I've been here in all weathers and you never know if this is going to be a big day, but you won't find anything if you're on your phone.' Good advice, indeed.

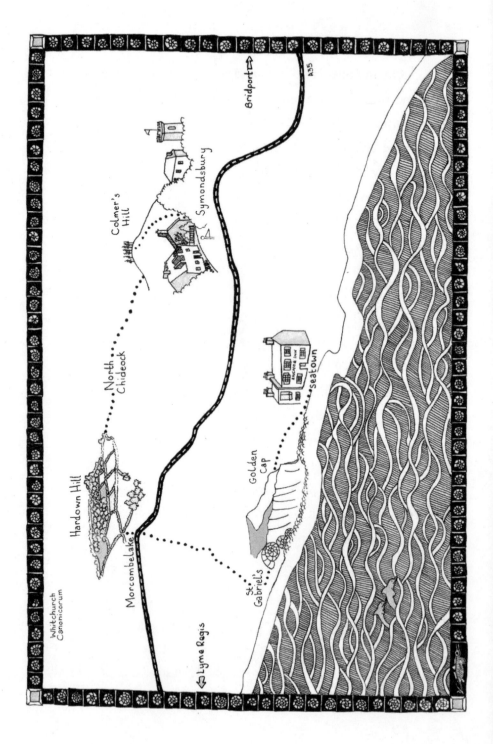

On any one day there are hordes of people doing this very same thing along this coastline, as this is true fossil-hunting territory. The beaches are sometimes so full it's a bit like Supermarket Sweep, except all the products are well past their sell-by date – by about 185 million years. Amazingly we found a fossil, an ammonite, the ones that look like coiled ram's horns.

This glorious part of Britain's coastline is Dorset, a county full of iconic places and a favourite location for millions of visitors every year, from fossil hunters to anyone who sat on the edge of their seats through *Broadchurch*, the gripping crime drama, and anyone in between. In this walk, I'm going to wander along the cliff tops where the secrets of our planet's past have slowly been unearthed over the centuries, as old dinosaurs have literally tumbled from the crumbling rocks. I will wander through beautiful valleys and explore small windy lanes, revealing picture postcard villages.

Those are the random thoughts buzzing through my head as the car slowly pushes west out of London, crawling in the early morning rush-hour traffic through Shepherds Bush. Cradling a coffee, I try not to think about the children back home. I'm missing them already, but this is the first day of filming, and, after ten months at home, it's time for me to be away (briefly) from my new baby girls and my little boy. And I need to converse in dialogue that extends beyond, '*Ooo yoooor soooo booooo–ti–ful. Look at yoo–ooo–ooo. Bah-bah-bah-bah–bah! Brrrrrrrrrrrrrrrrr. Buuuuuhhhh.*'

This coastline – never mind Dorset itself – is full of wonderful treasures, beautiful views and awe-inspiring sights. I especially love this walk for its combination of different elements: the little overgrown lanes, with chocolate-box cottages hidden away; villages that appear to live *in* the landscape around them, rather than having been plonked on top; the gentle, rolling hills and steep-sloped cliffs, where all kinds of animals – rabbits, foxes, badgers – may rustle in the undergrowth, while gorgeous sea-going birds soar and dive overhead; all with a history that reflects our nation's struggles at birth. I can't think of a better way to start this journey – it's a perfect introduction to the pleasures of walking in Britain.

I have had a fitful night's sleep at The Bull in Bridport, a small but lively market town. It's my first time in a strange bed after months of being at home, first pregnant and the size of a rhino and then, later breastfeeding the twins at all hours of the day and night (think British Friesian hooked up to a milking machine – that's what feeding twins is like). During the night, I kept hearing weird noises and thought it was the girls crying out. Despite this, this morning I'm raring to go, especially as now I'm out hiking again I can treat myself to a sausage sandwich. I feel as if I'm still carrying an extra little parcel of 'chubby' around the girth, but the next seven weeks of hiking should take care of that.

We've been warned to expect some cloud later on but it's a beautiful clear September morning. For a walker, cloud is no bother; for TV purposes though it's not great. We want the amazing views at the end of the walk to be at their best, so we need to reach them while the good weather holds. And that means an early start. Which I hate. But the light can be better earlier and the routes ahead are usually fairly clear for us, so we're not dodging scores of other walkers. Some of the places we are going to walk in the series are very popular. The Dales walk we do later in the book, on a summer's day, is said to be like Cup Final day at Wembley, it's so busy – and that's not too enticing when you're walking, let alone seeing it on telly.

A walk in these parts is never ordinary because as I said, you're walking through time – through the geological phases of the Triassic, Jurassic and Cretaceous periods. This is the spot where the 2m (6.5 ft) skull of an ichthyosaur was found by an exceptional 12-year-old girl, Mary Anning, back in 1810–11, a discovery that arguably sparked the long fascination that geologists have had with this coastline, which continues on to this day. Mary is also said to be the 'she' they're talking about in the irksome tongue-twister 'she sells seashells on the seashore'. And that's exactly what she did. The daughter of a local carpenter, Mary and her siblings, her brother, Joseph, in particular, helped their father collect and sell fossils to wealthy summer visitors and collectors. Fossil collecting was in vogue in the late eighteenth and early nineteenth centuries in England, at first as a hobby, but over time the science behind the fossils came to be better understood.

A few months after finding the skull, Mary discovered the rest of this ancient crocodile-like creature, in the end assembling an almost complete skeleton. She sold it to a rich landowner but it eventually it made its way to London's Natural History Museum, where the skull remains to this day. It was an amazing find and Mary discovered many more such fossils over the next twenty-five years. She is often referred to as the 'greatest fossil hunter ever known', but sadly, she was overlooked because of her sex and social class. In a society dominated by wealthy men, she was prevented from fully participating in the scientific community of early nineteenth-century Britain. Over her lifetime, however, Mary became very well-known in geological circles around the world, and yet, as a woman, she was not eligible to join the Geological Society of London and she was never published (a true sign of credibility), apart from when she penned a missive to a natural history magazine questioning one of its claims.

Paddy Howe points out: 'To make the discoveries she did, she must have been out in some terrible storms, and after landslides when the cliffs had been disturbed. She had a huge amount of determination and is a great inspiration to me.'

It must have been very frustrating to be Mary Anning in 1800s England. A bit like being David Attenborough today, with nobody listening. These bony discoveries were quite stunning to the nation back then. Most people in Britain still believed that the earth was only a few thousand years old and that species neither evolved nor became extinct.

'The world has used me so unkindly, I fear it has made me suspicious of everyone,' Mary lamented. She died of breast cancer in 1847. By the time of her death, geology had at least become a recognized science.

Now you might have thought that after 200 years of geologists scouring these beaches, this area would have given up most of its fossils, but this is the coast line that just keeps on giving. See these headlines:

In 2014: *'Gold rush: Jurassic Coast is packed with treasure hunters after ichthyosaur skeleton worth £15,000 is discovered during a Boxing Day walk.'*

And in 2008: *'Dinosaur fossil most complete found in UK: A dinosaur skeleton believed to be the most complete found in Britain has been unveiled before it goes on public display later this month.'*

Maybe I'll be lucky on my walk today and find more than a tiny ammonite this time round? As the crew set up, I suspect my mind won't really be on fossils for much longer. This is the unspoilt western edge of Dorset on the south-west coast and I'm heading to the highest viewpoint on England's south coast – the deliciously named Golden Cap. Just a little reminder – this is England's *only* natural World Heritage Site. And let's not forget *Broadchurch*.

Like the rest of the nation, I was absorbed by *Broadchurch* when it was shown on TV, hooked into the tense unfolding of its mystery, shocked at the revelations in the final episode and drawn into the bracingly beautiful scenery of its setting. Oh those beaches. I met some of the cast members at the National Television Awards at the O2 Arena back in January 2014. Jodie Whittaker (Beth Latimer) and I compared bumps – well, the *Daily Mail* compared our bumps anyway. Jodie 'showed off' her bump, while I apparently 'proudly paraded' my 'expanding belly' which didn't sound quite as glam to me. 'I'm carrying two,' I reminded myself the next morning. Throughout the night I tried to prise out details of the second series from Jodie and the others, but the cast were all very discreet and of course I couldn't ply them with alcohol otherwise we'd have made different headlines.

We begin the day in the village of Symondsbury. Sometimes when a camera crew turns up in a small village, people come out to stare, wondering who's there and why they're bothering to film in their little home town. Not in this case. Symondsbury is so pretty and picturesque, so crammed with history, that the locals are more than used to cameras there. In fact, it's so lovely that I wouldn't be surprised if they stop people who don't have their cameras out, wondering what's wrong with them.

I should mention the crew because they'll be with me every step of the way and I may talk about them every now and again. I'm with Eric today who's directing this episode for the walking series – and there's nobody better because he's local and knows the walk and the surrounding area like the back of his proverbial hand. Eric has a shock of white bouncy hair and a thick scouser accent. If there's ever a potential situation we always send him in to disarm everyone with his amiably sunny disposition. Jan's a big, hairy, lovely cameraman of Polish descent, sporting a lovely moustache. And Colin, the soundman, carries the big fluffy thing, the boom or microphone. Fran is the researcher who puts in all the hard recce work finding locations and writing up notes on everyone and everything, so I know what I'm talking about. By current TV standards we're a fairly compact team. One day Jan and I will be one person. Of course I could film the whole series with a smart-phone on a selfie stick, but it would look rubbish.

The pretty village of Symondsbury gets a mention in the eleventh-century Domesday Book. Like most of us, I know a bit about it from my schooldays – how William the Conqueror – William I – after his invasion of England in 1066, wanted to record the possessions in his new kingdom and so commissioned a complete survey of the kingdom of the lands, compiled in one big fat book. It's a fantastic record for social historians, a piecing together of the layout of our country from almost a thousand years ago. Of course, William didn't undertake it for that reason – he wanted to know how much tax he could raise from his new subjects. I don't suppose he got much money from Symondsbury, or Simondesberge ('berg' meaning a hilly barrow), as it was known then, where there were only thirty-one houses in 1086. Nowadays it's a bit larger, with a population of over 1,000, a lovely old school, a gorgeous thatched pub and some beautiful Georgian manor houses and idyllic cottages, but it's still surrounded by the same undulating hills that King William's surveyors would have seen.

I wander into the little churchyard, and take a peek into the old parish church of St John the Baptist, which is well over 500 years old. It has that evocative musty smell you get in country churches. I grew up next to one in a village in Rutland in the East Midlands and we used to play hide and seek behind the altar, so I know that smell well. I walk out towards the building that lies just along the lane to a nice looking café in a converted tithe barn, which Fran scouted out during her recce. It fulfils that wonderful 'two-in-one' duty – we can get food here *and* we can film here. I pick up a picnic lunch, and some tasty chocolate brownies to keep me going on the walk.

Chaz, the person who greets me and asks what I'd like, doesn't have a West Country accent at all – she sounds as if she grew up next door to our director, Eric. A smiling lady in in her forties, Chaz tells me about the village and the estate it's built on, while I sip my coffee. I'm particularly interested in the things I'll see on my walking route, so she tells me something of the history of Colmer's Hill, my first objective. It's named after the Reverend John Colmer, rector of the church in the nineteenth century. The infamous pine trees planted on the hill top, which make it so recognizable, weren't, in fact, planted by

Colmer, but by the Colfox family, who held the estate for years and planted the trees during the First World War.

I'm interested in why Chaz, a girl from Liverpool, is so far from home.

'I came here with my best friend after her mum saw an advert for a summer job in the *Liverpool Echo*, and packed us off,' she tells me. 'I think she wanted to get rid of us. I fell in love with the place, met my future husband and never went back. I stayed because of the place more than my husband to be honest. My best friend went home and she's still there.'

It's a familiar story: people fall in love with a place and never leave. Not just from other parts of this country, but from other parts of the world. In this particular enclave of Dorset, though, there aren't that many immigrants because there aren't a lot of jobs. It's quite an ageing population and there are lots of second homes which has caused a whole set of other problems for rural communities, when locals get priced out of their own neighbourhoods.

It turns out, from what Chaz tells me, that I'm in the hub of the Colfox estate, which still owns most of the land round here. They've been clever as they not only offer walkers a chance to get supplies before heading off on their walks, but they've also created this shorter walk which I'm about set off on, which picks up the main route just to the back of the café. I wave goodbye to Chaz and go on my way, my rucksack now bulging with goodies for later (mostly chocolate brownies, I admit). It's time to face my first uphill climb and I'm looking forward to the effort.

As every walker knows, you have to respect the owner's rights on the edge of the paths and lanes you walk along in the English countryside, but some definitely treat walkers better than others. Walkers rely on the landowners or their tenants to repair stiles and fences; but equally, it's important that walkers remember to abide by the rules and shut gates behind them and stick to the path, as much as possible, as much for safety as anything else. I'm glad to say that in this part of Dorset, the Colfox estate has looked after the land – and us walkers – very well.

Colmer's Hill is a well-known landmark, a proper classic hill formed by a quirk of local geology, thanks to its distinctive shape and the trees atop it. It can be seen from Bridport High Street and even out at sea, so it's no surprise that locals tell me that when they've been away, they know they're nearly home when they can see the hill in the distance.

People have been climbing Colmer's Hill for centuries. It's a bit of a steep climb to get to the top, but there's a perfect winding path here through the ferns . . . and what a great reward. There's a trig point in among the pine trees – and the view at the top, even though we're only 127m (417ft) high, makes the hike well worthwhile. You can see far across the Dorset countryside, over the surrounding fields to Bridport in one direction and out to the English Channel in the other.

While we're setting up for the shot on top of Colmer's Hill, Jan, the cameraman, seizes the opportunity to take one of his power naps, lying flat out next to the trig point, cap pulled down over his eyes, walking stick possessively clutched in his arms. He gently hums as we all discuss the next sequence. It's hard work lugging a huge camera round up and down mountains (even if you're Jan who is a big sturdy fella) – almost as hard has having a small child in your Bush Baby backpack. The camera fidgets less at least.

It's so perfect, I'm sure people must photograph and paint the hill and its view regularly – and, sure enough, we find two locals who do just that. Former postman and mackerel fisherman Doug Chalk is wearing a battered old Barbour that looks as if the pockets might be stuffed full of poached trout (of course, that's not the case). He's got a flat cap on, covering his baldness, and his two protruding front teeth have a gap in between them, resulting in what looks a permanent smile. Doug has been visiting the area since the 1980s and finally moved here about sixteen years ago. He lives in an old pub with his partner of twenty years and they apparently haven't changed a thing. There's still a pool table and a bar downstairs.

He readily admits he's obsessed with the hill and photographs it almost every day from his deck, as well as from other perspectives, He's even produced a calendar of his photographs, which he's brought along to show me. Doug spent a year photographing the hill, showing it in almost every kind of weather, sometimes with rainbows framing the hill (there's yet to be a drought in Dorset; this is England after all), and he tells me that he's made some changes to the garden so as to have the perfect view of the hill:

'When I first moved here I removed quite a few weed trees from the garden just so that I could have a clear view of it,' he explains. 'Now I have a viewing deck and can even see the hill when I'm sitting in my bath – and when I'm having a wee, I have a photograph of Colmer's on the wall and I can look directly out of the window at it too.'

I laugh out loud with Doug. 'You are a bit obsessed,' I joke. He's extremely passionate about Colmer's – but then most of the locals seem to be that way about this hill, as are the people who flock here every year. And it's not just photographers who have loved coming here. This iconic hill has also been painted thousands of times over the last few hundred years. Here at the top, I'm meeting up with local artist Marion Taylor, who's published a book, *Colmer's Hill – One Artist's Obsession*, of works by twenty-two artists who've adored this mound. I hardly need her to tell me why, what with these amazing views, but I still have to ask: what's so special about it?

Marion is sketching away and, while she does so, she explains why the hill and its surrounding landscape so fascinate her. She first visited this area twenty years ago and never left. She has a background in textile design, but now prefers to paint Colmer's Hill: she's painted it almost 200 times. Marion appears to be reassured and almost nurtured by the hill. Maybe it's the familiarity?

She turns out to be a dream interviewee (or 'contributor' as we call them in telly), responding naturally to every question and comment I make to her. Overly nervous contributors can be tricky and it's difficult to know if people are going to be any good when you shove a camera in their face. It's the researcher's job (Fran, in this case) to interview them over the phone and make a judgement call as to whether or not they're going to make good telly, but a telephone call usually doesn't faze people in the way a camera does. Thank God for editing. Marion, though, is a natural, happily ignoring the huge camera lens and fluffy boom overhead, attached to Jan and Colin, the soundman.

'The boom's in shot,' growled Jan.

'How wide are you?' asked Colin, referring to the size of the shot.

'I'm *that* wide.' Jan's big arms stretched out.

'Well, where am I meant to put the microphone?'

'Not bloody well there!'

'Ladies – calm down!' I chastise.

Marion explains the fascination that she and other local artists have with Colmer's Hill. For her, it's the trees that make it something special. She tells me that when the trees were first planted, the gardener on the estate used to carry full buckets up the hill to water them for the first month.

'Oh, it's not easy growing things up here, is it?' I say.

'No,' she responds quickly. 'And nor is it easy carrying buckets of water up here!'

As I leaf through her book, Marion talks about the paintings she especially adores and how the bracken turns a particular kind of rusty red in the autumn. I don't know much about art, but I definitely prefer contemporary work: David Hockney, Mark Rothko, Andy Warhol, Keith Haring. I adore most of British–Indian sculptor Anish Kapoor's work and, as it turns out, I like Marion's too. It reminds me of Hockney's Yorkshire Wolds collection.

It strikes me, as I sit with the lovely Marion on top of her hill (her grandchildren call it 'Nana's mountain'), that this must be one of the most painted mounds in the country. And it's only little. I know there are hundreds of hugely popular landscapes from the Lake District through to Constable Country that have been painted innumerable times, but is there a single hill anywhere else that has garnered so much artistic attention? Prominent artists Paul Nash and Fred Cuming have both painted Colmer's Hill, and their work appears in the book alongside several of Marion's own pieces. Of course, compared to Kim Kardashian's bum, Colmer's Hill is a drop in the ocean, but for one dinky mound to have made such an impact is quite impressive. It's definitely a favourite of mine now and I think it's largely to do with the distinctive pine trees planted at the top of the classic dome shape.

As I'm sitting here, thinking how nice it would be to bring my kids up the hill one day, I think what a lovely grandma Marion must be (and I have to make it clear that my own mother, Chrissi, is a fantastic grandmother, or *YiYi* in Greek). She doesn't look old enough to be a grandma: her dark hair has only flashes of silver threads running through it. She seems content and warm, with a sense of fun about her and her grandchildren see her every day; they run into her studio yelling her name, arms outstretched for a hug.

As I get up to leave, Marion casually mentions, 'When there's a full moon, a group of us have a shamanic fire ceremony on top here, and we throw our arms into the air and thank the universe for this beautiful spot and the nature around us.' I won't lie. It's a surprise. I didn't have Marion down as a shamanic worshipper. But then, what does one look like anyway?!

I'm genuinely sorry to say goodbye, it's been fascinating to talk to her, I'd love to stop and take a bite of my sandwich, but there's no time to linger – it's onwards and downwards! – so have to leave her there sketching away. I'd love to try those shamanic rites sometime, I guess I'll have to come back for the next full moon. This hill clearly has its own very special magic.

An old friendly looking golden retriever barks at me as I lean over a gate to peer nosily at an unfeasibly beautiful garden located at the bottom of the unnervingly named holloway, Hell Lane. A powder blue shepherd's hut sits in one corner, surrounded by potted plants; the spinach green lawn is trimmed to perfection, while dozens of handsome mature trees and bushes frame the vibrantly colourful flower beds. If this were at the Chelsea Flower Show, it would win Gold for Best English Country Garden. The pretty thatched cottage to the left looks as if Hansel and Gretel might be in residence.

'Hi there!' I call over the gate. 'What an idyllic spot – do you mind if I intrude?'

'Not at all,' comes the softly spoken reply. 'Come and have a cup of tea.'

Tim is one of those gentle souls with a yielding voice and kind blue eyes. He's a born-and-bred Dorset man, who's lived in this cottage for 20 years. He bought it from a friend of his father's. It's nice that it didn't get sold as a second home to be rented out or as a weekend place for an out-of-towner. That's common and also how communities lose their identity, with no one local living in them. Mind you, this is a bit more rural than I'd choose. There's no mains electricity and Tim tells me that he's just about to update the shed roof – to become solar powered, charging batteries by running off photovoltaic (PV) panels. The cottage has its own water source, a well, which Tim and his wife, Collette, use for showering and to flush the toilets.

'I think that's why my first wife left me . . . she got fed up with the shower running out of water,' Tim jokes. He and Collette have been married for three years.

As I chat to Tim in their gorgeous garden, taking in the

incredible views across the valley, Collette leans out of the kitchen half door listening in, looking very like a character from *The Darling Buds of May* or – actually, remembering I'm in Dorset – a Thomas Hardy novel. The thatched cottage, which is in the process of being repaired, has no top windows. 'You'd better hurry up Tim, it's nearly October!' I joke.

'I'm a builder and we always do our own jobs last,' he comes back.

The cottage was apparently originally used by smugglers who would come up from the coast at Eype in south-west Dorset, bearing their illicit goods, using Hell Lane as a secret route to get away from the excise men intent on arresting them. Tim shows me a book published last year, *The Holloway*, all about the lanes in this part of Dorset. Before I leave the cottage, I ask Tim what I should expect.

'Well, it's ancient and has a magical mysterious mood about it, but you should just go and see it for yourself. Ferns growing up the banks; it's all shady, it's nice. There's high-sided cliffs that are a bit precarious, they just crumble away, so watch out for the landslips – oh, and the graffiti etched into the walls. Faces, and strange things. There's an indent in one of the banks and a little shrine there to the Virgin Mary, with trinkets 'round it.'

Leaving their idyllic garden, I feel as if Tim has thrown me to the wolves. I start to negotiate my way down this narrow, dark lane moving towards a mysterious underworld – an ancient drovers' route which was the main road west before horse and coach travel came along. It's been used for centuries and the bottom of the lane runs deep below the level of the surrounding ground, thanks to the soft sandstone being eroded by floods and the footfalls of farmers, smugglers and pilgrims heading to the great shrine of St Wite in the village of Whitchurch Canonicorum. I can really feel the ancient feet that have tramped here before me – it's like some kind of ghostly fairytale pathway into the unknown. And I can picture the smugglers carrying their rum and other contraband under the cover of these trees and dense hedges. Just enough light leaks down through the canopy above to make out the ancient graffiti and funny carvings on the walls that Tim mentioned. Some prankster has notched the word 'HELP' next to claw marks scraping down the wall . . . Ha ha! Very funny.

'Thank God I've got the crew with me,' I think, otherwise I'd be spooked. Who knows what went on down these dark lanes?

In this area of Dorset, there are a number of holloways like this and they make a good backdrop for storytellers and authors. In the thriller *Rogue Male*, written before the Second World War, the hounded fugitive hero returns from abroad, fleeing foreign agents. He hides out in a lane, where his pursuers eventually catch up with him, which the author, Geoffrey Household, states is right here, on a descending ridge from the hill outside North Chideock. The novel became a bestseller in 1939 and inspired many spy-hunt thrillers from Ian Fleming's

James Bond novels to Frederick Forsyth's *Day Of The Jackal* – and even the Rambo books. It also became a Hollywood movie, TV and radio series and still sells today . . . all from a book based on this quiet, hidden pathway in the heart of sleepy Dorset. Some say the author's ashes were scattered here when he died in 1988, so the spirit of the Rogue Male may float eerily through this mystical hollow even today – what a thriller. Household wrote that 'nobody but an adventurous child would want to explore it'. Oh – and me. He forgot me, I think, as I head up the lane.

I meet four silver-haired walkers on the path. 'Oh, what are you filming?' they enquire.

'A new walking series for next year.'

'Oh, well, don't mention this spot – we don't want everyone coming here and spoiling the place!' They guffaw. I've never understood this attitude towards beautiful places, secret beaches or good bars and restaurants: why wouldn't you want other people to experience somewhere lovely? To enjoy what you enjoy?

Finally, I come out of the mysterious green tunnel and back into daylight. This is the village of North Chideock. Despite its pretty cottages, it too conceals a dark past: during Elizabeth 1's Protestant reign, the Arundell estate was the focus of Dorset's Catholicism. Several local men were tried, convicted and executed. They became known as the Chideock Martyrs and there's a memorial to them on the edge of a field here.

In the village there's another surprise awaiting me. Thankfully, my surprise has nothing to do with death or religion but rather to do with food – but not the usual cream tea found in this neck of the woods. Instead, waiting inside one of these cottages is celebrated local Japanese chef Shigeaki Takezoe, famous for his six-course traditional Japanese banquets which are cooked and served all from this unlikely looking location. There can't be many Dorset villages that can boast that!

'Hello Shige,' I say when I meet him, leaning over a split door as I peer into the tiny kitchen. 'What Japanese goodies are you serving up today?'

Shige is polite and charming to a fault; he hasn't lost his Japanese accent after almost thirty years of living here. Inviting me inside, he offers me some tempura, which is delicious – it's certainly more unusual than my chocolate brownie and sandwich combination from the café earlier today. As we sit at a pub-style table and bench in Shige's lovely garden, I can't help but think that the whole scene is a bit surreal. The tempura is exceptional, the weather 'brilliant', as Shige declares, and the entire experience really very unexpected.

I ask how he comes to be tucked away deep in the English countryside. He tells me that he met his wife, Diana, thirty years ago, when she came to teach English at the air cargo company in Tokyo where he worked. Later, Diana tells me, 'There were about fifteen men and me – they were very welcoming and friendly, but they drank a vast quantity of beer, whisky and wine in a short space of time. After about half an hour most of them were too drunk to carry on speaking English. There was only one younger man who still wanted to talk. He seemed quiet but interesting. I wasn't particularly attracted to him! His English was poor, but he had travelled to various places in Europe and Asia. He liked jazz and said he had a spare ticket to see Sarah Vaughan a couple of weeks later.

'From his point of view it wasn't an instant attraction either!' she adds. 'He just wanted to practise his English and thought I spoke really clearly.' Yet, true love was born.

The couple returned to the UK, where Shige taught Japanese while learning English at London University. After working for some years in Newcastle, Shige and Diana headed south, partly to get away from the cold wind – so bad that even Diana couldn't bear it. Sometimes 'you thought it would take the car door off when you opened it', she says. Shige just says, 'It's too cold for a Japanese person.'

Now they run a business from the cottage. He specializes in Japanese banquets – 'an extended hobby', he says modestly. He cooks for the nearby cottages and also delivers his food to the local community at large. There's a big demand as all kinds of people have moved to the area. As many come from big cities, they're used to eating a wider variety of food that is not normally found in out-of-the-way villages like this. Even so, there've been some hiccups, like the time the diners assured them they were familiar with Japanese food, but drank the tempura dipping sauce. It's 'delicious, but it is also very rich and not really meant for drinking, I was worried they would feel sick afterwards and ruin the rest of the meal,' says Diana. Luckily that didn't happen.

Shige and Diana also tell me about the time they had a famous actor staying in their cottage. Normally they like to greet guests at the front door so they only see the clean and tidy parts of the house; but the actor arrived with a birthday cake for his wife, so came marching from the car into the kitchen to put it in the fridge. Diana was mortified: 'I was feeding the children baked beans, surrounded by washing, including a muddy rugby and swimming kit, school work and other debris from the day.' The actor didn't bat an eyelid.

They're lovely, and I think it would be a real treat to stay at their cottages and eat Shige's delicious food, but I can't sit around all day enjoying myself: I've got a walk to complete.

'What is it you like about Dorset?' I ask Shige before I leave.

Shige says he likes Dorset because he loves dinghy sailing and regularly sails at the Lyme Regis Sailing Club. He also loves mountain biking. Diana loves walking along the cliff paths in Dorset and never gets bored of the views of the sea or of the rolling hills and farmland. Textbook reasons for living in these parts really, but valid nonetheless. I make my goodbyes to the couple and head off on my way.

I'm over halfway along my four-hour walk now, as I head up towards our second hilly viewpoint – the summit of Hardown

Hill. First I make a short stop-off to take a look at an ancient unspoilt valley that offers a couple of amazing stories as well as more magnificent views – that's the fossil village of Charmouth and the unchanged Marshwood Valley, surrounded on all sides by Iron Age forts. Standing here it's possible to see, off in the distance, Pilsdon Pen and Lambert's Castle, actually a hill fort. Closer to me is the Anglo-Saxon village of Whitchurch Canonicorum. It's a bit of a mouthful but it's home to a remarkable church, the St Candida and the Holy Cross, which still has the relic of the body of St Wite, which thousands of pilgrims visit every year. Sadly, not a lot is known about her. It's believed that St Wite saved local people from a Viking raid in 844 by lighting beacons from a hill much like the one I'm about to ascend. She was later murdered by more Viking raiders. St Wite's tomb is one of only two shrines with relics that Henry VIII didn't destroy following the dissolution of the Catholic monasteries in 1536 – the other is in Westminster Abbey.

It's possible to take a two-mile detour off our route to visit this church for those who fancy a longer walk. Aside from St Wite's tomb, the churchyard is also the burial place of the Bulgarian spy Georgi Markov, murdered in 1978 by a poisoned-tipped umbrella on the streets of London, a story so bizarre – albeit true – that it could easily have featured in the pages of thrillers like *Rogue Male*. The churchyard is also the final resting place of the bow-tied broadcaster Sir Robin Day, who first launched *Question Time* on TV. It's full of surprises this quiet little spot. Still, I won't be taking that detour today: I've got another hill to climb.

When people are watching my walks on the telly surely they know that I have a crew in tow? But when I bump into a family here on holiday from the Ribble, I've become separated from the crew and they seem a bit concerned: 'We always see you walking on your own,' they tell me. It's my fault: I marched on ahead while they filmed some old tractor. When I realize they're not with me, I reach for my mobile (yes, even here I've got a couple of blips of signal), but before I make the call I'm going to take the opportunity to have a pee in private.

If you're out for a longish walk, especially with children, you have to accept that at some point you're going to have to do what we call a wild wee. Or something else. When we're out filming, blurting out that you're going for a pee or a poo seems wrong somehow so we use codes to protect our modesty. 'I'm going to see if I can find any otters,' is Jan's favourite. I use: 'I'm going to water a tree.' Anyway I just need to make sure the cyclist passing by doesn't spot me crouching in the undergrowth watering this tree.

When we all catch up, it's time to film the summit of our second hill on today's walk: 'I've reached the highest point of the walk so far, at 207 metres,' I say. 'Across the small hedged-in fields, I can see Colmer's Hill behind us and now at last, looming above the sea, Golden Cap, our final destination, just ahead.'

Hardown Hil couldn't be more different to Colmer's: this

is a sprawling, high area with no defined bump. Hardown Hill rises above the villages of Ryall and Morcombelake and sits midway between Bridport and Lyme Regis; it qualifies as a 'Marilyn'. You may have heard of a 'Munro', meaning any hill or mountain higher than 915m (3,000 ft); well, a Marilyn (in punning contrast) is a hill or mountain with a prominence of at least 150m (492 ft). The flowering gorse is plump, thick and bouncy up here, a challenge to walk through as I deliver my piece to camera, but beautiful to look at. The air smells so fresh on this Marilyn – and no wonder. There are loads of pretty herbs, grasses and plants found here, with wonderful names like Potted shrimp garter and Spanking meadow. Actually I made those up . . . Oxeye daisy, Goat's beard and Corky-fruited water-dropwort (try saying that after a couple of pints) – they're all real. I'm no botanist but I've picked up a few things over the years and when you live in a city you really value the beauty of a place like this. A well-manicured London garden doesn't compare to a wild valley like this one. I take a deep breath and thank my dad: 'Thanks for making me appreciate our green spaces when we were on all those walks together.' You'll meet him on the Edale walk (Chapter 8).

St Wite's name crops up all round these valleys. As I walk into Morcombelake, I come across a spring named after her. This small stone well has been a place of pilgrimage for at least 400 years. It's believed that St Wite's Well has healing powers, specifically for problems with eyesight. A local scientific survey into these waters discovered exceptionally high levels of zinc – which is also used in many eye drops. Maybe that's its secret. I guess it's hard for us to grasp in these hard-headed days that something we now regard as an issue of faith actually has a grounding in fact.

It's a calm and peaceful place to stop and think for a while. Surrounded by meadows, all you can hear are the buzzing flies, the chirping crickets and the hum of bees as they fly about and it would be easy to stay here and do nothing but think. That's what's great about a good country walk: it slows you right down and lets you decompress. Coming to this ancient Dorset landscape, you realize that walking was once our way of life, long before cars and mobile phones; so I take a moment to enjoy the solitude. And then I see a beautiful bright red and burnt orange flower that I don't recognize and realize that I'm not alone after all. I take a photo with my phone and send it out into the Tweetosphere. Within minutes dozens of people are telling me that I'm looking at a Crocosmia, commonly known as a montbretia. They're good, my followers – and that's something that I wouldn't have been able to do even ten years ago.

My final stopping off point, before I head up for the big climb to the top of Golden Cap, is the sweetest little chapel in the now abandoned Anglo-Saxon hamlet of Stanton St Gabriel. A few dozen families survived here until the fifteenth century, but eventually the chapel inevitably fell out of use. All that's left today are the remains of this tiny chapel which, according to a twelfth-century legend, was built by a local sailor named Bertram, who had been saved from a sea storm and built the chapel in thanks, even though his new bride had died in the wreck. Even today, people still get married here.

As I'm walking, I come across another photographer, my second today. Stephen Banks is an amazing young time-lapse expert, whose incredible photos of the Dorset countryside by day (and particularly by night) have made the front pages of the nationals.

Time-lapse photography has exploded in popularity, thanks to sites like YouTube and Vimeo. It's a technique that shows the natural progression of time by shooting the same scene again and again over an extended period. When you play that sequence back at a normal speed, time appears to be moving faster and 'lapsing'. Some smartphones now come with time-lapse built into the options for their video cameras.

Stephen's Facebook page is called the Dorset Scouser – yes, he's another Liverpudlian who moved south because of the landscape – and he's been posting time-lapse films and photographs to promote the area ever since: 'To show a different side to Dorset. Not just old people sitting in beach huts eating ice cream,' he tells me.

His pictures are exciting and unusual, like capturing the International Space Station at night going over Charmouth to Bridport, where he lives. But he works hard for his art: 'I spend a lot of time driving to places at about three or four in the morning. You need patience and hardiness to the cold.' He has a curious looking bit of kit, which he tells me is called an 'equatorial mount' – it rotates at the same speed as the earth's rotation, so the stars in the night sky don't get blurred in the picture. Stephen's art is real proof, if any were needed, that this Dorset landscape has a timeless beauty that appeals to us all.

I sometimes wish I had more time with my own camera on these walks; it's brilliant seeing so much of the countryside but when you're filming time is always precious. There aren't many spare moments and sometimes things just fly by in a bit of a blur. This rolling landscape with its cliffs, valleys, fields, ponds and heaths is perhaps the epitome of the English countryside. Birds, butterflies, orchids, bees, hay meadows and heathlands are all around you here. And there's so much wildlife you can see on this rich coastline, such as all six species of the British adder (lucky us); red squirrels; Barrel Jellyfish, one of the largest seen along this coastline, roe deer, the only true native deer to Dorset; and Grey, Common or Harbour seals, which can be seen at Poole Harbour, Portland Bill or Chesil Beach.

At last, I'm facing the last climb of my walk, up the slope to the top of Golden Cap, our third hill viewpoint and at 191m (627 ft), the highest point on the entire south coast of England – 30m (98 ft) higher than Beachy Head and almost twice as high as the White Cliffs of Dover. I can't wait to see the views along the Jurassic Coast; while, on the top itself, there are also 4,000-year-old Bronze-age burial mounds. The route I've chosen is the steepest approach up Golden Cap. I'm arriving from the west side, along the coast path, heading east on my climb. Golden Cap's top was sliced off in the last Ice Age, but is eroding at about 1m (3.28 ft) every year; back in the Iron Age, when the burials mounds were fresh, this cliff would have been sticking out into the sea by a further 3km (2 miles).

It's this heavy erosion that makes this bit of the Jurassic Coast famous for dinosaur fossils like the ichthyosaurs and plesiosaurs, which swam in the Tethys Ocean here 165 million years ago. It's amazing to imagine what it must have been like then, with pterodactyls flying overhead like giant seagulls. There have been quite a few stories in the local press about aggressive seagulls swooping down on unsuspecting tourists and swiping their dinner clean away – even small dogs have come under attack. Imagine a 226kg (500lb) gull with a 12m (40 ft) wingspan and around 1,000 teeth bombing towards you. Hold on to your chips.

As I reach the top, I'm taken aback by the view, even though I knew it would be magnificent. Over to the west is Lyme Regis and the Cobb, with Charmouth in the foreground, while over to the east, I can see all the way along to Chesil Beach and beyond it to Portland Bill. Straight ahead is the English Channel and, miles further out there, France. Lyme Regis is bathed in spectacular sun, its rays streaming through gaps in the clouds. I ask Eric if I should use the term 'Jesus Rays', which is what these slices of sunlight are sometimes called: 'No,' comes the prompt response.

Looking out I can see why 'set-jetting' has become a real tourism phenomenon around here. I know from my own experience what an impact a TV series can have; when episodes of *Wainwright Walks* were first shown, the Cumbria tourist board would talk about the 'Julia effect', as they called it. There were a few pissed-off people who couldn't park in their favourite car park. In Dorset, the series *Broadchurch* has made a real difference to the local economy. Reports from the council show over 70 per cent of businesses reported an increase in turnover in 2014, the year following the first series, and half of the town's businesses make *Broadchurch* references in their websites or leaflets. Good on them. Chris Chibnall, the show's creator and a local resident, has said, 'I wanted to make a drama where something terrible happens in a beautiful place.' He certainly achieved that.

As I stand here, I think about the walk I've done, which encompasses the heights of three ancient hills, the lower depths of lush green valleys, secret hollows and sacred legends and now, at the end, offers this unrivalled view of England's only natural World Heritage Site. Golden Cap is a prize trophy of a walk and full of unforgettable views that can't help but put a long-lasting grin on your face.

All in all, it's been a good day. We haven't fallen behind schedule, the weather has held, the crew are happy and we managed to get a closing shot in glorious fading sunlight – the kind that casts a handsome glow over everything it touches. It feels good to be back and have the first walk in the can.

'You haven't lost it, Jools,' Eric chirps. 'Your energy levels are still up there.'

Speaking of energy levels, there's still one more treat in store for me down at the Anchor Inn – a refreshing pint of cider and a big plate of food. After a couple of snifters and a seemingly never-ending delicious dinner at the inn, we all start to chatter. We clink glasses, 'Here's to a Dorset cracker.'

Not only does this landscape embody the very essence of walking, but it's also packed full of history, wildlife and surprises. I didn't expect to eat authentic Japanese cuisine (prepared by an authentic Japanese man!) in the heartland of Dorset at the exit of an old smugglers route and I didn't anticipate falling in love with a diminutive hill that stands less than 130m (500 ft) high. Walking always throws up new experiences – it's never *just a walk*.

We all head back to the hotel after dinner. Only once I've taken a long hot bath, tweeted some fans who share a love of Dorset and tucked myself up in bed, I find I can't sleep. The mattress is comfortable – I'm exhausted from hill walking – and now back in reality, I can hear some classical music whining loudly through the walls from the room next door. It could be something I like (doubtful), I might hate it – I just don't know. I can't make out the tune, just the noise.

And all I want to do is sleep. I think of Jan who snoozed so easily stretched out on the hill top. Aa–aargh.

WALKER'S GUIDE:
WHERE TO STAY, WHERE TO EAT,
WHAT TO SEE, WHAT TO DO

To start off: I had an excellent bacon butty at the Symondsbury Kitchen (Manor Yard, Symondsbury Dorset DT6 6H6 – https://curatedby.theoutdoorguide.co.uk/symondsburyestates /brandfront/Symondsbury-Kitchen) to start me on my way.

To visit: The lovely town of Bridport, where I stayed: charming in its own right, but it also boasts West Bay, the beach where much of the key action in *Broadchurch* takes place.

To finish: A pint in the Anchor Inn, in Seatown (Bridport, West Dorset DT6 6JU), is the best way to finish off this walk.

To visit: The unique church of St Candida and Holy Cross in the magnificently named village of Whitchurch Canonicorum. Visible from Colmer's Hill on this walk and only a two mile detour from it, this is a 12th century church and the only parish church in the country to still feature a saint's shrine and relics, in true medieval style.

To spend the night: I stayed in the Bull Hotel (East Street, Bridport DT6 3LF – https://curatedby.theoutdoorguide.co.uk/ thebullhotel).

2

THE COTSWOLDS: THE CLEEVE HILL WALK

'Everything is within walking distance
if you have the time' – Steven Wright

I'm about midway through my Cotswolds walk when I reach Sudeley Castle, best known as the home and final resting place of Katherine Parr, the last, and arguably luckiest, of the six wives of Henry VIII – because she survived him. After the King's death in 1547, Katherine promptly remarried and moved to this magnificent residence, only to die one year later, aged just thirty-six, following the birth of her daughter, Mary.

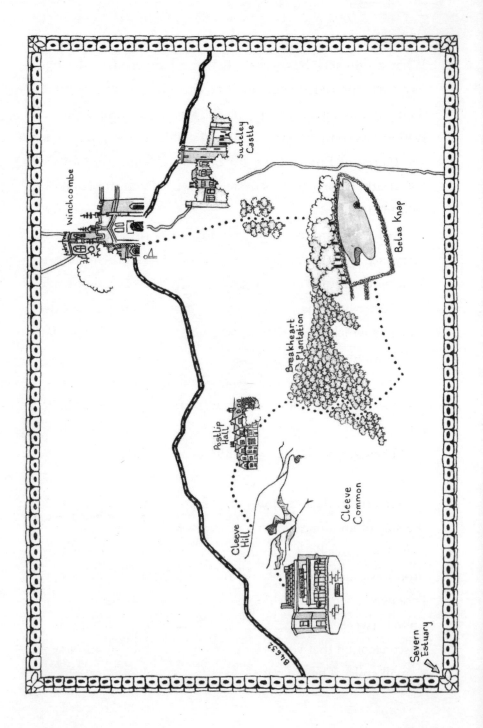

What a downer! Knowing what had happened to the five wives who preceded you, outliving the King, only to peg it at such a young age. It's a tragic tale, but there's more. One of Katherine's companions was the ill-fated Lady Jane Grey, who was Queen of England for just nine days, following Edward VI's death, before she was ousted by Mary I and subsequently beheaded. Ouch!

As I walk into the castle grounds, a surprising yet friendly furry face appears at a fence. And another. And then another. Sudeley has acquired some new residents it seems, hopefully with better luck that the previous collection of female royalty – llamas which the guests can rent by the hour and take for walks around the grounds.

'What's the difference between an alpaca and a llama?' I throw at Jan, the cameraman, who pretends to know everything.

'The size and the fibre quality. A llama is bigger,' he shoots back.

He's right. Again. Smart arse. The llama is roughly twice the size of an alpaca, with a coarse outer coat and fine inner coat. The alpaca has a fine single coat but, despite being smaller, produces much more fibre because it's been bred for that purpose over 5,000 years. Although an adult male llama can reach up to between 136 and 200kg (300–440lbs), there seems to be a misconception that you can ride them. Not true, unless you're a small child. They're only meant to carry about a quarter of their body weight. So when you read about 'alpaca and llama treks', don't be disappointed that you're going to be leading *them* around on a leash.

'Goodbye Oscar,' I shout over my shoulder (one of them *must* be called Oscar surely?).

I certainly didn't expect to meet llamas today, here in the Cotswolds. I knew it was going to be very beautiful, because even if I hadn't known the area well enough, the region appears with such regularity on our TV and cinema screens that you have to wonder if someone's earning a royalty – and if so, who? Americans love the Cotswolds, too – if you want to impress a visitor from overseas, but still be home in time to get the children into bed, then taking them to the Cotswolds always works, as they 'ooh' and 'aah' over the small, gentle hills, the gorgeous cottages, the stunning little villages and the glorious manor houses, hidden away down windy lanes. It's very domesticated and it's in easy reach of London – so it seems perfect to visitors from abroad. Is it any surprise that the Cotswolds holds such broad appeal? It's an Area of Outstanding Natural Beauty (AONB) that runs like a geological spine across six counties, from Somerset to the south, right up to Warwickshire, across 2000km² (almost 800 square miles). We're in the county of Gloucestershire, but right throughout are the famous rolling hills or 'wolds' that give their name to the region. These gentle-on-the-eye curving and undulating hills give you such a sense of peace and tranquillity, a real escape from frantic modern-day living. Provided, of course, that you're not rained on, as we had been.

Walking in the rain isn't much of a picnic, as we all know, but it's impossible to walk and film in the rain, so the crew and I had been stuck indoors while we waited for the clouds to disperse and the sun to shine before we started the walk. All that green has to come from something, I suppose. We Brits love nothing more than a chat about the weather, don't we? It's how we speak to strangers, usually, a cheery, 'Hot enough for you?' tossed out while we pass someone on a footpath. But it's no fun when you're at the mercy of it. Luckily the Ellenborough Park Hotel, where we'd been staying, gave me a room the size of a tennis court. Sadly I didn't pack my racket, but it was very handy for our production meeting as we tried to work out how to rejig things to squeeze two days of filming into one.

It may come as a surprise to some people, but almost no television programme, except for the live ones, is made from start to finish. Because of all sorts of things, such as weather conditions, the numbers of people involved, traffic, the need to have certain people from the crew together for a series of shots – for almost any reason you can think of – a programme is made in a round-about way, and gets pieced together by an editor in the edit suite. Luckily today, Josh is directing this episode and he's also the editor of the series, so one thing I do know about this particular walk is that every shot is going to be very, very precise because he edits in his mind as we go along.

The rain finally stopped and we were released from the grounds of the hotel. By that time, however, I'd eaten my body weight in cake and the local single Gloucester cheese, so was praying that I could still fit into my waterproofs.

The walk we've planned is roughly 10 km (6.6 miles). It begins in Winchcombe, then continues along a portion of the Cotswold Way, an approximately 160km (100 miles) route from Bath to Chipping Camden that runs along the Cotswolds escarpment, or 'Cotswold Edge'. From Winchcome, the route goes past Sudeley Castle, where I'm at currently, and on to an ancient burial mound named Belas Knap. The grand finale finds me on top of Cleeve Hill (I'll meet you in the Club House), the highest point in the Cotswolds, with sweeping views of the Severn Estuary, Wales and the Brecon Beacons in the distance.

While there are a number of towns that can lay claim to being the 'jewel of the Cotswolds', there's no doubt that the absolutely stunning Winchcombe is one of them. Small windy alleyways, little courtyard gardens, with classic English flowers, such as roses climbing out from beds of geraniums and trailing lobelia, all framed by that gorgeous honey-coloured stone make everywhere I look heavenly. Most of the villages and towns of the Cotswolds are built of the local limestone, which can be different parts of the colour palette, depending on where it's quarried. It's easy to see this in the west, with the silvery-white stone of Painswick, while, to the north-east, there's the golden ochre stone of Chipping Camden. It's an oolitic (from the Greek for 'egg') Jurassic limestone created out of millions of fossils, particularly sea urchins and it's familiar because you find similar stone in the Rutland villages where I grew up. Winchcombe's Vineyard Street, so called because it was the site of the original vineyards in the abbey's grounds, is almost too good to be true. Serried ranks of leafy-green trees line the pavements in front of houses that seem to glow in the morning sunshine. But I wasn't there just to gawp like a tourist, so we walked on to our first stopping point, St Peter's Church.

Situated in the centre of town, St Peter's draws many visitors, but most of them don't even bother to go inside. The chief attraction of the church is on the outside, high on its walls. It's proof that the stonemasons who worked on the church when it was being built had a sense of humour, because the grotesques are fabulous. Grotesques are the stone-carved faces on the side of the church; they're not gargoyles, which is what people usually think they should be called, because gargoyles perform a function on the building – they have waterspouts coming out of them, for rainwater to run off from the gutters, the gargoyles shooting it clear of the building without the need for ugly drainpipes. Grotesques perform no such function and are purely decorative.

There are forty grotesques on the church going back to the fifteenth century and many of them are supposed to caricature prominent locals of the time. There is one in particular, to the east of the porch, which seems to attract the most attention (and which features on most of the postcards I've seen in shop windows around town). Could it be because it resembles a certain Mad Hatter from *Alice In Wonderland*? Author Lewis Carroll, who lived in Oxford, did spend time in the Cotswolds, so could this carving have been what sparked his imagination to create one of the most memorable fictional characters of all time? Local historians insist no, that it's mere coincidence, but it still seems curiouser . . . and curiouser.

After this, I headed over an old stone bridge out of town. There are six major footpaths leading in different directions, but I knew I was on the right one. Luckily, everything's clearly marked with signs everywhere.

Winchcombe is the self-professed 'Walking Capital of the Cotswolds', and declares on lots of signs and properties everywhere that 'Walkers Are Welcome'. This is a countrywide initiative designed to give focus to towns and villages which are making efforts to attract visitors (around 100 places around the UK have earned the title) and to ensure that walkers who want to travel to parts of the country they wouldn't normally go to get the best possible experience. With lots of local enthusiasm from officials in the town, as well as local businesses, ramblers and wardens, Winchcombe's Walkers Are Welcome has got off to a flying start, so it was interesting to meet some of the people involved.

Sheila and Robert Talbot, who set up the group in 2009, have been working on it since Hebden Bridge, in West Yorkshire, organized the first Walkers are Welcome initiative, in 2007. It was, and remains, a time-consuming project for them, but it's reaping rewards and visitor numbers to the town are up. The group website helps walkers and other visitors plan ahead for their trip to the Cotswolds, while, on the ground, their network strives to devise walks available to all ages and abilities, and with a different slant to each of them. Sheila and Rob greeted us enthusiastically, but before I got to interview Rob I had three other tiny sequences to film. The couple watched on patiently as I explained where I was on the walk, pointed up to some signs and walked across a couple of fields. This took us a good hour-and-a-half – just to make a couple of minutes of telly.

I finally got the chance to ask Rob, dressed in a red anorak, about Walkers Are Welcome.

'We do strive to make sure there's a walk for absolutely everyone, for every interest and occasion,' he explained. 'We have, of course, the major long-distance walks, as well as the shorter walks like yours, today.'

There is the Winchcombe Way, a 67.5km (42 miles) walk that I say to Robert sounds interesting, as well as, of course, the Cotswold Way itself (164km/102 miles) which passes through the town. The Cotswold Way would be fun to walk as you would catch sight of the various locations used in the adaptation of J.K. Rowling's novel *The Casual Vacancy*. Five Cotswold towns were in the end used to take the place of the book's fictional Pagford: Bisley, Minchinhampton, Northleach, Painswick and Burford.

'We have every kind of walk you can think of,' Rob continued, as we trampled through the stubble on the field. 'There are trails with wheelchair access, historic walks, heritage walks, nature-themed walks, circular walks, figure of eight walks, geology walks, guided walks, self-guided walks, night-time walks, jam walks, riverside walks – and we even have a walking festival.'

That's a lot of walks (what is a 'jam walk'?, I mused, before realizing that it must mean a fruit-picking walk), but I wanted to know more about the walk that I was on.

Rob was delighted that I wasn't just wandering about the lanes by the village, but striking out to Cleeve Hill. He told me that there are tremendous highlights along the way. The first of which, Sudeley Castle, wasn't too far away and was, he said, a spectacular sight as it absolutely dominates the valley.

'But I must say, Julia, you're in for a real treat today. Belas Knap will completely spook you, the woods are magical, and to finish at the top of Cleeve Hill is a perfect choice!' Phew!

The walk towards the castle is down a splendid avenue of lime trees. When I see such views, I always wonder what it must have looked like when the trees were just young saplings and about the men who planted them knowing they wouldn't live long enough to see them come to their full glory. Inspired horticulturalists really are green-fingered superheroes doing it for the good of mankind, because they never get to see their best work.

Llamas apart, Sudeley Castle is as spectacular close up as it is from a distance. There's a chapel to one side, and a ruined building behind it, all adding to its gorgeousness. The roof even has battlements, so it looks like a castle from far away, but a house from the top down.

The castle is still a private residence, which is amazing. What do the owners, the family, do when the place is shut up at night? Go roller-blading down the long corridors? Potter about in one of their nine gardens? You wouldn't want to be the one who got into bed and then wondered if you'd shut all the windows downstairs; it'd take half the night just to walk about checking.

As I walk around the sun-covered walls of the castle, archivist Derek Maddock tells me a more uplifting story than that of Katherine Parr and Lady Jane Grey. And he's quite uplifting himself.

'Centuries later,' he told me, 'this was the home of the fabulously wealthy Emma Dent, who spent a fortune on restoring the castle, which, by the mid-1800s, was in ruins. She was also your classic Victorian eccentric and philanthropist who worked tirelessly to help the local community. She built a water supply for the town, provided almshouses and a school, built a church – she was a powerhouse.

'And one thing that will certainly interest you, Julia, is that to say Emma Dent was a keen walker is an understatement. She'd take off whenever it pleased her – and each time she went into town in the evenings, to run her night school, she hired a boy carrying a lantern to guide her home so she didn't stumble over the sleeping cows.'

Yeh. You've got to watch out for those lazy Friesians . . .

I like the sound of her. 'So she recorded her walks?'

'Meticulously,' Derek says, producing one of her notebooks – and another small object. 'She even had this device made, an early pedometer, to measure the distances she covered.' He shows me a glass display bell with what looks like a pocket watch hanging inside.

I compare the 'Dent Machine' with my state of the art Garmin VivoActive Smartwatch. Mmm. Hers is prettier, I concede, but I'm quite keen on my digital gadget.

'Yours is more functional,' Derek agrees.

He hands me the notebook and I read from it. *The Diary Of Emma Dent*, with all the words and phrases just as she wrote them. It's full of hilarious entries. Derek's right: Emma Dent was quite a character. I read:

26th December 1859
The servants had a party consisting of husbands, wives, and children. Marianne and I for their amusement dressed up; she in the Bears Dress and I as old Christmas – we made an

appearance on the balcony of the Servant's Hall and were greeted with thundering applause. We lowered Christmas presents amongst them and disappeared as we had appeared.

It must have been like Cirque du Soleil . . .

11ᵗʰ April 1861
I think it is one of my greatest blessings to be able to say I never know what it is to feel dull or lonely! but in society have often thought 'oh when will this be over'!

We've all been there, dear. Have another Cosmo . . .

26ᵗʰ July 1878
A dreadful storm came on at 4 o'clock just as we were going into the long room – at 10 minutes past 4 it killed a cow in the Boilingwell Orchard and our poor Tom Shotten who was carrying the milk was struck down into the hedge and narrowly escaped with his life . . . I opened the billiard room window and looked out – a flash came from over Postlip which seemed to be coming direct upon me – when it suddenly turned attracted by the lightning conductor. With it came the thunder sounding like a hundred cannon balls! The lightning struck the tower loosening several large stone of the dungeon!

That actually sounds quite scary.

> *December 1881*
> I find I have walked during the year about 700 miles! We have 'entertained' since March as follows – At Breakfast 175 times, At luncheon 386, at dinner 252 and At tea 1,058 times.

That's a lot of tea . . .

> *16th January 1887*
> I find last year I stepped 1,075 miles, my guests were at breakfast 284, at luncheon 468, at dinner 380, at tea 645.

A little bit less tea . . .

> *December 1895*
> I have walked 1,200 miles, my guests were at breakfast 416, luncheon 482, dinner 615 and at tea 2,109.

Best mileage yet! Go Emma!

It's difficult to imagine how exceptional Emma Dent was in her day, what with her wry sense of humour and her extremely unconventional ways. Women didn't even have the vote (it was generally thought, by men, that we gentle folk just weren't up to the hard task of thinking and that Parliament would be ruined if women got the vote). Women had no rights at all really and were very much under the control of their fathers or husbands. It wasn't until 1918 that we were finally deemed capable enough to vote. But only if we were over thirty and owned a home. It took another ten years for us to get the same voting rights as the men.

I covered a story for *Countryfile* a few years back about three other extraordinary women, Jane Inglis Clark, her daughter Mabel, and Lucy Smith. Without the resolute determination of ladies like this, I probably wouldn't be writing this book or walking these walks.

Jane, Mabel and Lucy formed the Ladies Scottish Climbing Club in 1908, created so they could walk alone. Before that a man was a vital and compulsory addition if you were a woman who liked to hike. Women walkers then were expected to wear suitable clothing as well, which included long tweed skirts and even hats. I had a go at this up in Scotland where I had the pleasure of meeting a ninety-two-year-old lady called Rona Weir, one of the original members of the Ladies Scottish Climbing Club. If ever there was an advert for the outdoor life, Rona was it. She looked remarkable and kept up with us all day; the only thing she didn't do was a bit of rock climbing. I had a go during this visit, wearing the full nineteenth-century garb – and it was a nightmare. My boots got hooked into the long skirt as I tried to climb and I lost my hat less than a couple of metres up. No wonder some ladies dissed the uniform – never mind climbing, those clothes were lethal. I nearly broke my neck just walking through the heather.

I mentioned that women were expected to dress in a certain way to protect their modesty but some members would apparently dart behind a boulder to change into trousers before their excursion and on their way back, before returning to the village, they changed back into their skirts behind the very same boulder, as if it had never happened. A passing shepherd caught them in the act one day and said to the ladies on their way back down (in a thick Scottish accent): 'Ooogh aye, you've returned for your decency have you?' What a long way we've come and what a long way we have to go! I'm sure our Scottish ladies and women like Emma Dent didn't realize quite how pioneering their actions would prove to be for us.

I thank Derek before setting off again. Our leisurely walk today may not have impressed Emma Dent, but at least we don't have to go far before these spectacular views open up before us. We're now walking alongside fields, heading towards the woods at the top of a slope. For this section it's the drystone walling so typical of the Cotswolds that guides our way. One often recounted fact is that this stretch of wall runs for more than 9,600km (about 6,000 miles) – longer than the Great Wall of China – but you can't see it from space. It's impressive to think that not only have these walls been here for so long and form such an integral part of the landscape, but also that they're surrounding us, helping to give the landscape that contained, homely feel that so appeals to visitors.

It's a short downhill walk through the woods, with beech

trees of various ages and sizes around us as we descend. A
lot of the Cotswolds is broken up into patches of woodland
around large areas of grazing. That's down to history – and,
in particular, the boom in sheep-farming that meant wool was
exported across Europe from here. It was from these very hills
that the first truly wealthy people in the country came – the
wool merchants who made fortunes out of the wool trade in
the Middle Ages. Wool became so important to the economy
that a chair stuffed with wool – the 'Woolsack' – has been (and
still is) the seat for the Lord Speaker of the House of Lords
since the fourteenth century (and it's not to be confused with
the Woolpack in *Emmerdale*).

These dark woods, in which I am now stood, have been
here for centuries. The woods are leading us up a fairly steep
climb on to something really special - an amazingly vivid
reminder that this area was inhabited long before the Tudors,
the Anglo-Saxons and even the Romans. When I reach the
top of the hill I see a huge grassy hillock on the edge of large
open fields; the grassy knoll rises from the ground, with stone
doorways leading down into the dark ground beneath. It's
enormous; over half the length of a football pitch, with gently
sloping sides to enclose it. This is the monument called Belas
Knap. It's what's known as a Cotswold Severn Cairn. There
are other examples of monuments like this built around the
edges of the Severn Valley.

Bathed in the dark and mysterious past, this extraordinary

Stone Age monument is over five-and-a-half thousand years old and was built by the ancients as a place to bury their dead. During the excavations carried out in the 1960s, the remains of at least thirty-eight adults and children were uncovered from a number of chambers that line the sides. Despite the best efforts of archaeologists though, the real purpose of Belas Knap remains a puzzle. Here, we're meeting up with local artist and archaeological illustrator Liz Poraj-Wilczynska, who's dedicated most of her adult life to imagining what may have inspired the ancients to create this extraordinary mound.

As I've already said, it can be incredibly hard to find exciting experts, whether they're geologists, geographers, historians, or archaeologists, to interview on camera. Liz, a nice-looking woman in her forties, with penetrating warm sky-blue eyes, I'm glad to say is *not* one of those people. And she's a woman – hurrah – as it's also hard to find contributors who are female. They usually tend to be blokes, very often big, hairy ones.

It's interesting to hear Liz explain what her job as an archeographer is. She trained as an archaeological illustrator, specializing in reconstruction drawings for professional archaeology publications. Since then, she's used her knowledge to explore Belas Knap as it fascinates her. I don't think I've ever met an archeographer before, but Liz is extremely knowledgeable. As we walk up and onto the barrow, Liz starts to tell me what she's learned about the place.

'Despite its importance as the earliest evidence of human activity,' she explains, 'very little is known about it. This is a place of priests and people; there are four stones in the forecourt that were here before the barrow, so it is a site that's been in use for a long time.'

We reach the top and she points at various sections. 'The barrow is orientated north–south. At the north end, there's a false entrance, where the bodies of five small infants and a young adult male were found. In another chamber, we have twelve individuals, bones and skulls inside, but one of them is articulated – it's all in one piece. It's near the entrance, sat in a crouched position – that's interesting for us.'

'Why is it sitting?' I ask, already intrigued.

Liz says she doesn't know but ponders the question. 'Possibly it's one of the last ones put in. The bones were taken in and out many, many times for part of their rituals.'

She leads me down to the edge of the barrow and says, 'Right down at the end is a really low chamber, with two adult male skeletons and some flint artefacts.' Also at the far end is another chamber. 'The South Chamber has one burial inside it. It wouldn't have looked like this. The entrance would have had big stone slab on top and the stone slab would have had to have been taken off to put the bodies in.'

I'm fascinated. 'Does that mean it was a more important person?'

'Not necessarily,' she comments. 'And we can't be completely certain about the excavations, either, as we're not sure whether they were recorded completely accurately.'

She leads me over the top of the barrow. 'On the west side, the chamber had the remains of up to fourteen different people – pieces of them, not necessarily the whole skeleton. Some of the women and children had been hit on the head. They'd had a very sad end. We don't know exactly what happened to them, but it was certainly quite violent.'

It's quite hard to imagine such violence when you're in such beautiful and peaceful surroundings.

Liz takes me on to another entrance, where she says, 'I have actually slept in this one.'

I'm more than surprised. It's just a dark, dank hole with stone benches.

'You've slept in here?

'Yes, as part of the project.'

'Okay, dedication is one thing; obsession is another. Why?' I ask.

'I wanted to understand about the quality of darkness here at night,' Liz explains, 'and to see the chambers when they were lit. The project is about how people might have used this barrow at night-time, because it would have looked completely different.

'Imagine what it would have been like to have walked up the hill to get here at night, Neolithic people coming that way with burning torches for their ceremonies. We find evidence of a lot of burning here; Belas Knap means beacon hill. The forecourt, with a fire burning in the centre of it, would have been a very different place, a place of feasting and activity.'

'And you slept in here alone?'

'I couldn't get anybody to come with me. Even my husband won't.'

I wonder why . . .

'It was an amazing experience. There was a low hum from the wind blowing across the open mouth, displacing the air inside it. The barrow itself does make some extraordinary noises; just before dawn, it has this tremendous sound, like a crack that goes through it. It's probably the stones warming as the sun comes up.'

Liz goes on to tell me that on that night she'd had a dream about Neolithic people gathering around her at the barrow and, when she woke up, she'd come to the conclusion that she was being given permission to explore the barrow. After that, she felt she could start this project, looking at what is important about this landscape, why this particular spot was chosen. The weather must be one reason: it's a place of extremes, both hot and cold; also, because of the damp air from the river valley rolling up to the hills, it's prone to storms and lightning.

'I think that the lightning may be one of the most important reasons why this barrow is here,' Liz speculates. 'In the Neolithic, they would have thought that was completely fantastic – a bolt of bright light hitting the ground, the gods communicating. And after the storm, a beautiful rainbow, perhaps.'

I'm transfixed by Liz's stories of Belas Knap. I want to know where her fascination with it began.

'I've had a long love affair with the barrow,' she tells me. 'When I was young, we lived in Cheltenham and my four older brothers used to come here on their bikes, but I wasn't allowed to. When I got my first car, when I was seventeen, this was the first place I came.'

'It's very theatre-like,' I say, looking around the forecourt.

Liz is 'playing' the wall in front of me like a xylophone or Latin American *güiro*, running her right hand fluidly over the rocky fissures, her silver rings and bracelets chiming out musically in the hollow we're standing in. 'It amplifies the sound.' We stand and look around together for a while, silently absorbing the atmosphere.

Well Belas Knap's left me totally spellbound and silent, which doesn't happen very often, but it's by no means the end to the magic in this route. And as I need to forge ahead on the next stage of my walk in order to reach the highest point in the Cotswolds, I say goodbye to Liz and thank her for being so brilliant.

It is interesting to speak to an artist like Liz. The Cotswolds has its fair share of associations with artists and celebrities, including people who live here, as well as those who write about it, from J.K. Rowling to Jeremy Clarkson, Damien Hirst to Kate Winslet. They all, no doubt, share a passion for this beautiful part of England, but there's a composer whose love of this landscape earned him – to my mind – the greatest possible accolade. A walk named after him. That is the guttural-sounding Gustav Holst Way. A 56km (35 miles) walking route, trailing from the church where his mother played the harmonium, through beech woods and past villages alongside the River Windrush to the church where Holst was himself organist, created in the great composer's honour – and I'm going to walk along a short portion of it now.

Holst is probably best known for his orchestral suite *The Planets*, composed in the early years of the First World War, and, in particular, the stirring theme 'Jupiter', which was taken up as the Rugby World Cup anthem. In the late 1800s, young Gustav would often cross these hills, practising his beloved trombone. One story goes that he was chased out of a field by an angry farmer for frightening his ewes – and even causing them to go into labour! It must have been some tune.

But pretty soon, it's time for me to part ways with the Gustav Holst Way, which goes in a different direction to where we're going, so I peel off to and continue on along the Cotswold Way. Once again, it's time for a dramatic change of scenery. That's what I like about the Cotswolds: the landscape can alter rapidly, even if all you've done is crossed over the brow of a hill. Now I'm entering the dense woods of the romantically named Breakheart Plantation: it's like stepping into the past as what we see today has probably been like this for centuries. The woods are full of oak and hazel trees. Not only does their heavy canopy block out much of the daylight, but it also deadens the sound so that there is an eerie quietness. I feel like I'm on the set for *The Lord of the Rings* or *Game of Thrones* and that I must speak in hushed tones, for fear of alerting orcs or wood elves – it's great!

I pull up my hood as it's started raining again, but as we're under a lovely awning of trees, it's not too bad. Still, it's not good enough for Jan, who wants to make sure the viewers know that it's raining (he cares about you readers, too, but there's not much he can do for you). He takes a close-up shot of a very green leaf, dripping with rainwater, but he's not happy. Reaching into his pocket, he pulls out a bottle of water, which he splashes over the leaf to get the 'perfect raindrop'. Jan is a former art student, you see.

In the past, much of England would have been covered with forest like this and it's great to be able to walk through the wood, because it is very much like taking a walk though our island's story. Oak trees have always been important in Britain's history and not just because Charles II, in the seventeenth century, climbed up one to hide from the Parliamentary soldiers trying to capture him. The ships of the Royal Navy, from the time of Sir Francis Drake right up to Lord Nelson, were built of oak. Henry VIII's warship, the *Mary Rose*, which sank in 1545 (and which was salvaged nearly 450 years later) was, of course, also made of oak. It's amazing to think that the frame of the ship could last so well underwater, but then some of our oak trees themselves last for such a long time; there's at least one in the country that's over 1,000 years old.

It's not long before I start walking downhill again and then we're out of the woods and rewarded with a lovely view of the sloping fields and rising hills, one of which leads to my ultimate destination. It's a gentle and steady upward climb from here on my ascent to Cleeve Hill. On the way up and just past these farm buildings, is another key landmark on our route, Postlip Hall. It's a superb Grade I-listed manor house. Though much of it dates back to the seventeenth century, parts of it predate the Norman invasion. In 1970, it was snapped up by a housing association and adapted to enable eight households to live in way that works as a self-sufficient community, maintaining both the house and grounds. They live private lives but act communally to work on the house and grounds; today, the community is very much closed.

It is an interesting way to keep alive a lovely old building that might otherwise have fallen into disuse or even have been knocked down. In addition to the big house, in the grounds are a chapel and a lovely old medieval barn, used as a venue for weddings today. Postlip Hall has given people the option to stay in the countryside by providing affordable housing and jobs and that's a good thing.

This fabulous walk has led me over open hilltops, across

streams and through woodlands, immersing me in one of the country's most fascinating and precious habitats – limestone grassland, where the lime-rich soil supports a wide range of diverse plant communities. Over half of this wildflower- and butterfly-rich natural resource is within the Cotswolds and some of the finest examples are here on Cleeve Common, just on the other side of the estate.

I'm keeping an eye out for some flashes of colour provided by local butterflies – the blue wings of a Chalk Hill Blue or the metallic green wings of a Green Hairstreak. Really, who comes up with these names? I don't manage to spot one, although I do catch sight of some orangey-brown Small Coppers, well-named as they're small and orangey-brown. I like these little butterflies because they're quite territorial and the male will attack other insects if they get too close. Imagine being attacked by a butterfly – it's hardly the stuff of nightmares. Or is it?

Cleeve Common is a wide expanse of public land, the largest common in Gloucestershire. Not only does it provide a beautiful end point to this walk, but it's also one of the wackiest commons I've encountered. You see, the common is not just a stretch of open land; it also happens to be a golf course. So people are out walking their dogs, stretching their legs, and dodging golf balls!

Because we are so behind schedule, due to the lost day, the reshuffle and the continuing rain, we need the help of senior ranger David Stevenson. He escorts us to the bits of Cleeve

Common that we need to film in a hurry in his special access vehicles. I get a great photo of the crew balancing precariously on the back of the truck as we bounce up the pathway. I'm sitting comfortably in the passenger seat of Truck One, because sadly there isn't room for me in the back. Shame.

'Before we start, the common has some interesting by-laws that need to be observed,' David explains. 'No swearing, gambling or beating of carpets.'

I'm somewhat surprised by that last one – I had no intention of beating my rug – I wonder what that's all about? He doesn't know why they banned carpet thrashing, but does tell me that the fine for breaking the by-laws, when they were introduced in 1891, was forty shillings (£2).

In today's money, that's about £220, which seems quite steep. While I'm thinking about this, David goes on to explain the history of the common.

'What makes the Cotswolds unique is the bedrock band of Jurassic limestone that runs from the south of England all the way up to the north-east. And the Cotswolds is its most prominent outcrop. Where we are now, Cleeve Common, is its highest point. So what we have here is limestone grassland that's quite poor in nutrients, but perfect for grazing sheep.' And there are plenty of them around us. Up until this point, I must say I haven't seen many animals, apart from the llamas and the odd cow. Thankfully not sleeping, unlike Emma Dent. 'And there's the connection with the wool industry that brought so much wealth to this region from the Middle Ages onwards.'

Obviously I knew about the wool connection, but David has much more to say.

'The saying went that the best wool in Europe was English and that the best wool in England was from here. And it was the Cotswold breed, in particular, that was probably introduced by the Romans. Their fleece was luxurious and noted for its strength. You can spot them by their white or mottled faces, plus they have a calm and easygoing nature.'

The breed went into decline in the eighteenth and nineteenth centuries as wool manufacture moved north when the Industrial Revolution brought about new methods of processing the wool. But enthusiasts today have restored several flocks to the hills and now Cotswold Lions (as those same enthusiasts call them) are well established again. I can't help but think these sheep look a little bit funny because as a way of showing the quality of the fleece, farmers leave fringes ('well-developed forelocks', I'm told) to grow over the sheeps' faces, covering their eyes.

By now we've made it towards the old sheep-dipping pond. 'Because of its low-fertility status and fantastic setting, it was simply set aside as a place for grazing sheep, and public recreation,' David continues. 'It's also a designated site of special scientific interest, for the number of rare plants and animals, including snakes.' Oh, let's hope we don't run into any of those adders or grass snakes. I'm not good with them – they are genuinely one of the few creatures that make my skin crawl.

The dipping pond is not really a pond, but a long trough leading to a round pool, all lined with stone. David goes on to explain that, obviously, dirty sheep wool doesn't sell well on the market, so before the sheep were taken off for sale, they'd be brought here and led through fences to the trough, where they were pushed through. Really dirty sheep had to be hand washed because the dirt wasn't just cosmetic; it could harbour bugs that could, in turn, infect the sheep. The clean sheep would then clamber up the sides to dry out.

David tells me a bit more about the limestone grassland. He says that it is confined to the south and east of the country, where it's drier. The largest site in Europe is on Salisbury Plain, which isn't that far from here. It's also, sadly, disappearing as land use changes and new farming techniques bring about different pressures to the soil. In the fifty of so years from 1935, 80 per cent of the limestone grassland in the country had gone. We must, David tells me, look after what's left.

Now it's time for me to make the final part of my journey and that's the ascent to the top of Cleeve Hill, which I can see clearly in front of me. First, though, I have to navigate my way up bumpy, densely grassed ground. Taking extra care where I step, I feel I'm edging ever closer to the top of the hill and the wonderful views that await me, but then I find myself in the middle of the golf course. There's been a golf club here, hugging the side of the hill, since 1891, and perhaps it's because there are no physical boundaries between the players and the general public that Cleeve Cloud Golf Club is said to be the friendliest in Britain. Pierce Brosnan paid them a visit last year – I don't suppose he'd mind if I said 'hi' if I caught sight of him today.

Time for some of Josh's humour. He has a plan for this bit of the TV programme and hands me an old golf club. Now I don't play golf but this is a fairway wood not a driver . . .

'Excuse me - can I borrow one of your golf clubs?' I ask a father and son walking through.

'Erm, yeeess,' comes the hesitant response.

Josh's idea is that within this episode I tee off and nearly hit another person walking across the course, highlighting the bizarre nature of Cleeve Hill. That person will be, by the magic of television, me. Hilarious.

'Hey you – off the fairway!' I shout to myself.

'Sorry!' I yell back at me. Then I take a swing and miss atrociously, so I ask the man who kindly lent me his club to take the shot for me. That way, on the close up, I'll look like a pretty good golfer. Now who's laughing?

I'm nearly at the top of the hill. I can see it there in front of me. Just before it, though, is a single, lonely tree, known rather imaginatively as 'Single Beech'. It's a beautiful tree. Its top blown sideways by the wind, like some mad frizzy hairstyle, the tree is surrounded by a low wall – to keep the animals from nibbling the bark, I suppose. Twisted and bent by time, this is the highest tree in the Cotswolds. Further off, to the south-east, is the dewpond, which is a remarkable feature; one like it has been there for centuries. It's a water hole for wildlife to drink from, yet there is no natural running water up here. The pond simply fills from the rainwater that falls on the limestone plateau, so, as long as it's placed in the right place, it will always have water in it. I'm told this dewpond (which has been restored with a modern lining to prevent the traditional clay lining from cracking) only ran dry when firemen pumped out the water to rescue some goldfish that had been dumped there.

But my true goal lies ahead of me, and after a few short strides up the slope, I reach the trig point that marks the highest point in the Cotswolds. I'm only really 330m (c. 984ft) up, but it's still very special. The old English name for this hill is Cleeve Cloud or 'lump on a hill'; maybe something's lost in translation because 'lump' doesn't really do it justice. This view has been tantalizing me throughout my walk, with glimpses of what it would be possible to see from such a high point. On a clear day, you can see all the way to the Brecon Beacons in Wales; closer in, I can see Cheltenham Racecourse, and the River Severn. Before – and surrounding that – and stretching out to the west, as far as I can see, is a gorgeous multi-coloured carpet (alas, no beating, I'm still under the by-laws of the common) of fields, hedges and small woods. It's tranquil and gentle countryside the Cotswolds and this is a fitting place at which to finish my walk.

It's also one of the most unusual summits that I've reached. Usually a summit climb, no matter how easy, requires some sort effort and that means you have at least one thing in common with the strangers you might meet. You've all made the walk. Not up here. The thing we're sharing as we all stand together is the view: three septuagenarians sit on a bench in front of me, a young couple stroll by holding hands, a few lost golf balls are scattered around the grass. The only thing that would make it stranger is Oscar the llama up here on a leash.

Most good walks end at the pub and this is no different. We grab a well-earned pint at The Rising Sun, which actually faces west. I'm not complaining, as there's nothing like a moment to reflect on a satisfying afternoon's walk sitting in a pub garden. Our journey today has captured a flavour of what this whole wonderful place has meant to people through the eras and I can bet you anything (oops, there's another by-law broken) that they would have felt every bit as exhilarated as I am, sitting here. When you consider that the Cotswolds covers such a great area, this relatively short walk has still managed to cover many of the things that make this region so appealing the world over. We've also managed to peek behind the chocolate box image that the Cotswolds is so associated with to see something quite different – such as its mysterious and somewhat dark history at Belas Knap, the absurd and humorous grotesques carved on to St Peter's Church and possibly the oddest golf course I've ever come across. And sitting here, cider in hand, looking out over this stunning vista makes today's walk – without doubt – utterly perfect and complete.

Now how would Emma Dent put it?

Pedometer tells me I have walked six-and-a-half miles this day. I crossed numerous fields, some woods and two hills. I saw one church, met several llamas and visited an ancient site. It rained. In 2016 I consumed: 1,003 cups of tea and 38 pints of cider.

WALKER'S GUIDE:
WHERE TO STAY, WHERE TO EAT,
WHAT TO SEE, WHAT TO DO

To eat: Excellent local lunches can be had at the The White Hart Inn (High St, Winchcombe GL54 5LJ).

To visit: Sudeley Castle is a must and this walk's starting point: a stately home with llamas, once home to Katherine Parr (Henry VIII's last wife's), and to walker and lady Emma Dent (Winchcombe, Gloucestershire GL54 5JO – http://www.sudeleycastle.co.uk/).

To finish: This walks ends up at The Rising Sun (Cleeve Hill, GL52 3PX), where you can see me on film finishing a satisfying pint.

To visit: The eerie Neolithic site of Belas Knap, also featured on this walk. The Cotswolds might seem cosy and familiar in parts, but Belas Knap is a reminder of how ancient and extraordinary England's history is (Charlton Abbots GL54 5NL – http://www.english-heritage.org.uk/visit/places/belas-knap-long-barrow/).

To stay: We stayed at the Ellenborough Park Hotel in Cheltenham (Cheltenham Spa, Southam Road GL52 3NJ), which not only put us up but also did us a good lunch on the day filming was rained off.

3

ANGLESEY: THE SNOWDON VIEW WALK

'Bwrw hen wragedd a ffyn'
(Welsh proverb: It's raining old wives and walking sticks)

The third walk finds me out west on the beautiful island of Anglesey, perched on the north-west of Wales on the edge of the Irish Sea. It's a long way from London. A pretty long way from anywhere.

Although this is a series about walks, I'm starting my visit to Anglesey on a boat. I've been on this boat before, when I

was filming a series called *Wonders of Britain*. The guys, Tom Ashwell and his business partner, Phil Scott, run a boat company called RibRide offering adventure boat tours around the island, and are great. Conversation, though, is a bit limited when you're bouncing along with the sea spray in your face, but it's a great way to arrive on Anglesey. The sky is a bit grey this morning so the view and the waterline just fuzz into one, but I'm feeling refreshed after my sea salt facial.

The last time I was in Anglesey was in my role as the President of the Camping and Caravanning Club a couple of years ago. The Camping and Caravanning Club was created by a chap called Thomas Hiram Holding, a London tailor who loved camping and cycling. At its first camping expedition in Wantage (don't ask me why) in 1901, there were just six members. Today there are over half a million and past presidents include Captain Robert Falcon-Scott (Scott of the Antarctic) and Sir Robert Baden-Powell (founder of the Scouts). I'm obviously a bit younger and still alive, which helps, but I'm also the *only female* president in the club's history, which I'm quite chuffed about. I was very honest when I accepted the post: for me it isn't all about camping; it's about having a spirit of adventure and an appreciation of the great outdoors. But camping is great for the soul and research shows that families who camp together are happier people. As long as I have access to a hair dryer, I'm one of those happier people, too.

Anglesey as an island has a very different feel to the

mainland. It's known for its beautiful sandy bays and the dramatic cliffs facing the Irish Sea, but it's separated from the mainland by the Menai Strait, although there is a bridge, the first large iron suspension bridge in the world, built by the engineering genius Thomas Telford in 1826. Before that there was no fixed way to reach the island except by ferry, so, when cattle (the main source of income on Anglesey in the eighteenth century) had to be taken off the island for sale in the inland counties or in London, they had to be driven down to the water's edge and then made to swim across. Swimming cows! With the infamous Swellies, caused by rocks near the surface and the different tidal effects from each end of Anglesey meeting in the middle of the Straits, this water is tricky enough for expert human swimmers, so can't have been that easy or safe for the cattle. So tricky is the crossing that Lord Nelson (whose statue stands on Anglesey, facing the mainland) believed the waters of the straits to be among 'the most treacherous in the world' and that anyone who could sail there could sail anywhere in the world. So if you're up for some Royal Marines-style training or want to teach your cows to swim, you know where to go.

Coastal life is vital to Anglesey; the economic links to Ireland and mainland Wales, tourism (Anglesey's coastal path stretches for 200km/125 miles around the island), and food. One of the sites I'll be visiting today has to have special permission from Her Majesty the Queen to operate and sells its products to none other than the President of the United States. And then there's the seafood . . .

These are all reasons why I am arriving by boat – to show how important that link, between the islanders and the water that surrounds them, actually is. Once Tom and Phil's boat has dropped me down on a stretch of beach called Tal y Foel, I'm ready to start my walk. This is going to be a stroll of just over 9km (6 miles) along the coastline, featuring some of the best views of Britain's mountains you could wish for.

Even if you wanted to, and frankly who would, you can't escape the views, because the sight of Snowdonia across the water dominates almost every glance. Who'd have thought that, if you really want to see Snowdonia at its best, you actually should come to Anglesey? The mountain range is laid like one of those long mountain height charts. That view is going to be there pretty much all the way through my walk today, as I trek shoulder to shoulder with Snowdon. It's been quite a while since I've visited Snowdonia, and, with the children being so small, it will probably be quite a long time before I do so again, but it's an exciting place.

Walking by the sea is easy. Not only is it flat – as long as you keep the sea to the same side of you the whole time you're walking, you can't go the wrong way – but there are some spectacular contrasting aspects in almost every direction, with the sea, the land and the distant mountains of Snowdonia. There's clean air here, too.

Standing on the beach looking out I start to contemplate the complex waters of the Menai Strait. What's striking about them is how these are real deep sea waters full of wildlife. I can see herons, oystercatchers and curlews pecking around in the sands looking for food. Now, I'm on my way to meet Jess, who works for the Sea Zoo Conservation Centre on the shore here. The staff nurture baby lobsters and seahorses and then release them into the wild. What an amazing job to have! I want to know what you have to do to become a seahorse nanny, lobster wrangler or whatever they like to call themselves!

Jess is a lively twenty-five-year-old from Nottingham, although she looks younger with her brown hair pulled back in a ponytail. Jess studied Zoology and Marine Zoology at Bangor University and got a work placement at the Sea Zoo Conservation Centre and then luckily was taken on full-time here after she graduated. She's very excited to be on telly.

'Have a look in here,' she says as she shows me what she's doing on the beach, gesturing towards the plastic containers that look like paint tubs, which contain baby somethings. 'I'm just about to release these. It's part of our programme to improve the yearly output of juveniles to try and maintain and improve current local populations.'

It turns out the containers hold baby lobsters, which look like . . . well, tiny lobsters. These miniscule opaque creatures are just a couple of centimetres long, but you can make out all of their features, including their minute claws. Jess tells me that, in the wild, less than 1 per cent of the eggs that a female lobster carries will make it to adulthood. The staff at the Conservation Centre are releasing anywhere from 200 upwards back into the sea every year. The greatest threat the young lobsters face is from other lobsters, as there are no other predators, but lobsters are very territorial and can be cannibalistic in crowded conditions, although fortunately they can regenerate lost claws, legs and antennae. So these little guys need to be released in different locations. Once they're in the sea, it will take them between five to seven years (depending on the water temperature and how much food there is in the area) to grow to a size for selling on to restaurants and shops. It is illegal to land or sell a lobster with any tail damage, which means schemes such as v-notching the tails ensure females will safely remain in the breeding population for the next few years. Local lobster stocks have gradually improved over the last decade, aided by the juvenile releasing scheme and an increase in the legal minimum landing size to 87mm. I've been out on fishing boats with lobster fishermen and they actually measure the creatures with a steel ruler before landing the catch. Well, they did in front of me, anyway.

Jess hands me a bucket of baby lobsters to release.

'Off you go, little Lazurus,' I cry (I know, first Oscar, now Lazarus – I have a thing for unusual names). 'God speed!'

Jess also tells me about the seahorses they are breeding. This threatened species is made up of fascinating little creatures: they are monogamous and pair for life, changing colour when the pair greet each other and the male carries the babies, 'pregnant' for seven months of the year. Hmmm, now that would have been easier.

The centre is one of the only places in the *world* to have successfully bred the native short-snouted seahorse, which is vital as populations of seahorses worldwide are under threat from collectors of both living and dead seahorses and practitioners of Chinese medicine. The world demand for sea horses and sea horse-related products is vast with over 77 nations trading 25 million sea horses each year. As the marine fish keep their shape when dried, many are sold as souvenirs or are ground into powder form to treat all sorts of ailments, for which there are viable medical alternatives. Even more tragic, despite being notoriously difficult to keep in home aquariums, thousands of seahorses are also sold as 'pets', resulting in huge numbers dying quickly from poor nutrition, stress or disease.

It's lovely to be involved in something like this. 'Thanks Jess,' I say, wishing her good luck with her babies.

When you're older, the miracle of life seems all the more astonishing, especially after a struggle. The centre's ground-breaking work and the miracle of the tiny lobsters gets me thinking about my own IVF experiences. Being pregnant at forty-four with twins is a bit of a jaw-rattling experience, I can tell you; you reach every milestone with a huge sigh of relief, and then cross everything in anticipation of what's coming next. When my girls, Xanthe and Zena (Greek names, of course), were born last year, I couldn't quite believe it. I still can't.

The sea here is a real way of life for the people who live on the island and that's reinforced just a short walk along the strand from the Sea Zoo Conservation Centre. The ugly pipes that I can see sticking out of the wall along the edge of the beach, as I walk, are significant. Her Majesty the Queen owns the coastline and charges a nearby factory rent to use this, the purest of seawater and behind the gates, across the road, is a husband-and-wife-led operation making the freshest, purest sea salt, Halen Môn (Welsh for 'Anglesey Salt'), salt that is now sold around the world, from Pakistan to Tokyo. It's proved so popular that the President of the United States – yes, Barack Obama – has Anglesey Sea Salt sprinkled on his favourite chocolates. Personally, I don't get the salt-with-chocolate thing. I love chocolate, in fact I'm addicted to it, but I like my chocolate creamy and sweet. Don't mess it up with salt! It'd be like sitting Professor Green next to the Pope at a dinner party – it's an odd mix and probably won't work.

The salt factory and visitor centre in Anglesey is now eighteen years young and employs twenty local people. After spotting a niche in the market David and Alison Lea-Wilson have struck gold, so to speak, and it all started when David took a pan of salt water from the strait and boiled it down on the Aga. In 2014, Halen Môn joined the likes of Champagne and Parma Ham, when it earned the 'Protected Designation of Origin' status. What about that!

This is certainly an industrious stretch of beach. As I move on, I don't get far before I come across Shaun, the owner of his own Oyster and Mussel company here. There's a reason Anglesey provides such surprisingly rich pickings and it's down to all the clean water that washes in and out of the Menai Strait with the daily tides. This ebb and flow, bringing in masses of suspended matter for the mussels to filter out, makes for some of the best growing conditions for mussels in Britain. Shaun farms bed-grown mussels, which grow slower and are, therefore, hardier and very flavoursome – especially the smaller ones, which are the sweetest.

When I meet him, Shaun is bending over to pick up a very heavy looking pallet, bursting to the brim with mussels, which he then carries to his tractor.

'Hello there,' I say, 'That looks like it keeps you fit and healthy.' And he does look very fit and healthy, with broad shoulders and a smile to match.

'Certainly does,' he agrees. 'That weighs about fifty kilos.' All the mussels are hand-gathered, he tells me, before being taken back to be washed and packed.

'And do you actually like mussels?' I ask.

'Well, I did and then I introduced them to my wife,' he says wryly. 'She was very enthusiastic and started cooking them every day for dinner and it went on for weeks. Anyway, that put me off 'em for a while. I think I'm just about ready again to eat them, but probably no more than once a month for me.'

I ask him where he sells his mussels to. Abroad?

'No, they're all for the UK, especially in the summer season.' Shaun tells me he supplies lots of local places here on the island and in mainland Wales, adding that 'they go as far afield as Hull. I deal with wholesalers, but the distributors could take them to all sorts of places and I wouldn't know.'

Shaun is a man of strong views, some of which he expresses to me later when I ask him about the purity of the water in which the mussels are grown: 'Spread shit on the land and it's called fertilizer; in the sea it's called pollution.' He studied marine biology at Bangor University and got his masters with the intention of getting a job in the tropics, but twenty-one years ago, a small-scale local farmer sold his fledgling oyster business to Shaun. About fifteen years ago Shaun decided to work the long-disused mussel beds, although he had to build his own mussel dredger to get the beds up to scratch. He knows this isn't a family business and that his sons aren't likely to follow in his footsteps. One, Luke, is at university, studying biochemistry and molecular medicine. ('Yeah,' says Shaun. 'Everyone goes quiet when they hear that.') Ioan, the younger one, is determined to be a Michelin-starred chef and is doing work experience at a local restaurant that I'm going to be visiting later, The Marram Grass Café, which already has a great reputation.

I carry on along the beach, but this time look across towards the enormous castle looming up in front of me. It's the World Heritage Site of Caernarfon Castle. Now I remember my school history lessons about King Edward I and his castle building activities in places like Harlech, Conwy and, on Anglesey itself, Beaumaris, from where all the inhabitants were evicted so the castle could be built. They were rehoused in Newborough, which I'll be passing through later (only in Britain could a place be called 'new' when it's 700 years old). These castles were all designed to exert English control over Wales.

Caernarfon really is a castle-and-a-half. Built with more than a nod to the Roman fort that stood just outside the town (there was a Celtic fortress here even before that), the castle itself is a powerful symbol for Britain as a whole. Since the time of Edward I, and the crowning of his son in 1301, every Prince of Wales has received his title here. In 1969, it was Prince Charles's turn to be invested here by his mother. The story goes that Edward I promised the Welsh people he'd only give them a prince born in Wales, who spoke only Welsh, before producing his infant son, although no one really believes that little piece of theatre's true any more. Speaking Welsh is important here: the townspeople of the city are known locally as 'cofis' (pronounced 'Covi') and today Caernarfon folk number as the biggest collection of Welsh speakers in all of Wales. Here, Welsh is a living language: it's taught in all schools and for almost three-quarters of people it's their first language.

As my mum was born in Wales, you'd think I'd have an affinity with the language – but no, I've always found it difficult. For instance, just a few miles from here is a town with the longest name in Europe – Llanfairpwllgwyngyllgogerychwyrndrobwllllantysiliogogogoch. That's fifty-eight letters, including a quadruple 'l' – now that's just silly! The town existed on the Menai Strait before the Romans were here, but during the nineteenth century the worthies of the town changed its name as a gimmick to become a tourist attraction after the railways brought new prosperity to Llanfair PG (as it's known for short).

At this point, I'm a couple of miles into my coastal walk and apart from some sticky mud on the beach, it's been an easy stroll along the coastal path, following the beach, with the clean sea air filing my lungs. It's very beautiful, but the history on the banks opposite is a reminder of what happened here, centuries ago. I turn right off the pebbly stretch of beach, walking up some steps to climb over a stile into lush green fields. I cross the edge of the field to Cae Mawr farm, where I turn left down a lovely long track, lined with overhanging trees.

I'm going to delve back into the island's distant past. The impressive and imposing natural barriers – the mountains of Snowdonia and, more importantly, the waters of the Menai Strait – led to Anglesey being one of the last places to fall to Roman occupation.

Archaeological discoveries on the island in the 1940s – made when the RAF were extending a runway – helped reveal the importance of the island's past, showing that people travelled from all over Britain to take part in religious rituals here. To help me understand this part of ancient history and how – given that there are no written records from the Celts themselves – the story has been pieced together, I am meeting up with local archaeologist and historian Neil Johnstone.

'When the Romans finally made it across in AD61,' Neil tells me, 'it was just along here that they arrived, in some flat boats for the foot soldiers and the cavalry swimming alongside their own horses.' Better that than swimming with cows, I think. He adds that the Celts were lined up, ready to confront them and terrifyingly, as far as the Roman soldiers were concerned, the Celts had, among their ranks, women. Never underestimate the power of an extremely pissed off woman, as the saying goes . . .

'I understand that the Celtic women frightened the lives out of the Roman soldiers,' I remark.

'Yes, the Roman historian Tacitus famously wrote about the wild-haired Druid women, who were dressed "in their funereal clothes", screaming and carrying torches and how their frenzied spectacle stopped the soldiers dead in their tracks. But in one single battle that took place here, with an overwhelming army, the Roman soldiers not only wiped out the ancient Druid order, meaning that Anglesey was taken, but went on to establish a base here and then cut down the groves of sacred oaks where the Druids worshipped. After that, we hear nothing about Druids in British history.'

I want to hear more, but Neil tells me: 'Little is known about the Druids, a spiritual order of priests, due to the fact they never wrote anything down. It seems they stirred the greatest resistance to the Roman occupation of Britain, but their knowledge and traditions died here on that fateful battle day.'

Interestingly, the Romans only ever banned two religions: Christianity, and that of the Druids. That shows how powerful Druidism must have been for the local people and how much the Romans feared it. The force of the Roman attack suggests that Anglesey may have been especially sacred to the Druidic order. At the same time Boudicca – the Warrior Queen whose statue guides her chariot on Westminster Bridge near the Houses of Parliament – led her people in rebellion against the occupation and successfully took the Roman city of Colchester (called Camulodunum by the Romans) in Essex, while most of the army concentrated their efforts on defeating the Druids in Anglesey.

Neil goes on to tell me that the Welsh women must have made a lasting impression on the Roman conquerors, because one later married Magnus Maximus, who, in the fourth century, became the Western Emperor of Rome (according to Welsh legend), so they 'loved us and fought with us', he says somewhat patriotically. We've all been in relationships like that . . .

As we walk, I look over to the left where I can see the view that has kept me company for the entire walk: the estuary in the foreground, Caernarfon Castle across the Menai and behind it Snowdonia (including Snowdon itself, although its peak is slightly obscured from here). It's an imposing combination of contrasting colours on what is now a sunny day: the lush green flood-plain fields in the foreground, the blue band of Menai waters and the distant greens of the Snowdonian hills.

I thank Neil for this interesting insight into the history of the area and then begin to walk on until I come to a river, the Braint. Here, there are the largest stepping stones I've ever seen which I'll use to cross the water. If I fall between them – and the gap's pretty wide – then the top of the stones would be at least waist height. I love stepping stones; they bring out the child in me, but these are quite ridiculous. It's as though a giant has dropped them here for his or her own personal use. Actually, it's just because the Afon Braint is now tidal and the stones stand up very high when the tide's out and become submerged when it goes out. In other words, choose the time you cross here carefully.

Right after I make the crossing, I see the house that I'm actually aiming for hidden in the trees; it's a white painted cottage with a stone roof that looks out over the river and the stepping stones that I've just crossed, the holiday home of Maurice Wilks, who died in Anglesey in 1963 and is buried in the local churchyard. Wilks was the Chairman of Rover, the car manufacturer, but that's not why I'm here, and why I'm snooping around in the hope of spotting something rumoured to be in these parts. Seventy-five years ago, he also engineered, designed and built the very first Land Rover, right here on this spot. There are rumours that the fields around the farm could well be hiding one of Anglesey's most surprising secrets, a buried national icon – the prototype Land Rover. These days, Land Rovers pop up all over the world, and in just about every environment – more than two million have been sold since its debut at the Amsterdam Motor Show in 1948. Why is this so enticing? Well, I have a confession to make. I love the outdoors as you know, but I'm also a petrolhead. I've loved cars since I was a dot. On road trips with Mum and Dad, I could name the make and model of *every* car in sight and, as soon as I could afford it, I enlisted the help of a car journalist to help me track down my dream car – a (second-hand) Porsche 911 Carrera 4. I have been in love with the shape of the 911 for ever – I think it's because my first car, a VW Beetle, was a hand-me-down first from my mother via my sister. Now, with three baby seats to accommodate – I've gone the Land Rover route, too. When Maurice designed that car, he had no idea what he was creating and how enduring his design would be. And I'm sure he didn't think his perfectly engineered utility vehicle would end up being the motor of choice at the school gates!

As I walk up a little green lane, I'm on the look-out for Chris Davies, who helps run the local transport museum, Tacla Taid. And when I finally spy him, I'm not disappointed – although it's the car he's standing by rather than Chris himself that's caught my attention. That said, he is a big bloke who obviously works out and could lift this Landy right off the ground.

'She's lovely,' I say, flashing a huge grin as I touch the bonnet of the handsome-looking old car.

'That she is. A 1955 Series 1 Land Rover. A real beaut,' Chris explains devotedly.

'Can I have a go?' I plead, walking completely forgotten.

'Of course you can. Hop in.' And I do. No need to ask me twice.

'Whooooo!' I shout above the very noisy two litre petrol engine, as we nearly career off the narrow road into a ditch. I'd forgotten there was no power steering in 1955!

My favourite thing about this car is the individual wipers for each side of the windscreen which are powered from the main battery. I lean across Chris to turn on the wiper on his side, twisting the little butterfly-shaped switch towards me. The wipers squish across the screen. *Magic.* I don't normally like vintage cars, but this is an unexpected treat. And it's one of the first ever Landys – you don't get cooler than that.

This has been an unexpected and most pleasurable detour, but it's time to get back to the reason I'm here – the walk! Now back on my own two feet I'm off towards those dunes – you never know, I might even find myself a car hidden away. But at the very least I'll have a sit-down and a cup of tea; the question is, where? Ah – I'm in luck!

You wouldn't know it from the area we're in – it's hardly in a bustling metropolis – but not only is there a café just off the main road here, it's no greasy spoon either. In fact, The Marram Grass Café has recently been listed in the nation's *Good Food Guide* – and it's attached to a caravanning site.

Thanks to a couple of unlikely Liverpool lads, Ellis, the chef, and his big brother Liam, the business head behind the operation, the tin-roofed café has been transformed into a very successful and attractive local restaurant, with a lovely trailing vine and lots of hanging baskets. These lovely lads have a real appreciation of this area, of the kinds of foods that come from Anglesey and its waters and they use them extensively in their restaurant.

Ellis and Liam invite me to sit at a table with them and sample some of their dishes while we talk. They're good-looking boys, both sporting Musketeer-style goatees; they have big personalities and equally big smiles and they talk ten to the dozen!

'Most days we change the menu,' Liam says. 'But the theme's keeping it local, mostly Anglesey based.'

'We make the most of what's on offer,' adds Ellis.

I ask them how they managed to grow the business and to get the reputation they now have.

'Bribes,' they joke. But in all seriousness, the quality of the produce they receive from their suppliers is what Ellis says makes him 'a better chef', proving the brothers' passion is all about what's on their doorstep.

The Marram Grass Café evolved from something the brothers originally did to help their dad: he wanted to have the caravan site and there was a 'little greasy spoon' on the site. They wanted to keep it simple, so didn't change the building, but just started serving food to people locally. They knew what the farmers grow on their land and that's what determines their menu.

When I chat with them, they gently rib each other about which of them is the most talented, good-looking or clever – and yet they both manage to be confident without being cocky. Sometimes when you come across this sort of breezy assertiveness, you think 'what a cocky so-and-so' – but not with these two, no way. They will be stars, I'm sure.

The boys have definitely got something going on, an amiable charm and warmth that makes them perfect restaurant frontmen. There's a third brother, Conor, as well; he's an actor who appears occasionally when he's not in some theatre production. Plus, of course, there's Shaun's son, Ioan, working there.

'He's doing what I used to do,' says Ellis. 'Both granddads cooked at home, so we were making jam tarts, breakfasts . . . I loved it. When I was twelve, I went to a college on Saturdays, rather than playing football with my mates.'

When they made it into the *Good Food Guide*, the brothers' photos were taken for the *Guide*'s press release announcing the new edition. The story made it into the *Liverpool Echo*, and the lads' nan saw it. 'We think she bought an *Echo* for everybody in the street to have a look,' says one of the boys. It was an unexpected moment for them, as they didn't even know the inspectors from the *Guide* had been in.

I'm given a few delicious things off the menu to taste, including an incredible chocolate carrot cake pudding called the Potting Shed, in recognition of the restaurant's origins – it was once a garden centre. If you're in the area, The Marram Grass Café is worth a visit. As most of its dishes are seasonal, you can bet that whatever I ate won't be on the menu, but you'll enjoy whatever it is they do serve you. Anyway, it's time for me to head off and the lads have promised I'll see them at the end of my walk to taste some of Shaun's tasty mussels.

My path back to the coast leads down a small track between fields. The land here is very open and flat; there's not a lot of distinguishing features, but once I'm past the fields into open country I keep an eye out for anything interesting – and, as if on cue, I spot some wild horses. What a land of contrasts this is. I'm only a kilometre or so out of Newborough and I've gone from Land Rovers and fine grub to the sight of something beautiful running free.

The horses are encouraged to run wild here, as part of the efforts of improving biodiversity, roaming all over this area, including down to the beach. That they can do so is down to the way the sand dunes have been kept at bay, both by the pine woods and also by the special grass that grows in the dunes that literally knits them together, preventing them from collapsing and drifting inland. This grass, called Marram grass (which explains the name of the restaurant), was planted here in the sixteenth century, at the special behest of Elizabeth I, after the sand dunes started sweeping across the farmland surrounding Newborough. The dense, grey-green Marram grass benefited the town in other ways as it could also be woven into sturdy mats, baskets and ropes; while the dunes themselves became home to thousands of rabbits, whose meat and furs also provided an income for the locals. That's how to turn a potential disaster into a success!

To get to the beach, I've got to slog up the dunes, never an easy thing to do but good for the calf muscles – at least, that's what I am telling myself. It's worth it when I get to the top because it's stunning: now that's a sea view and a half. There's the mouth of the Menai pouring out into the sea, with the mountains rolling down to meet it. Looking south, you can see Snowdonia, followed by the distinctive blue silhouetted peaks of Yr Eifl (The Rivals), a double bump of bosomy hills, leading to the smaller peaks of the Llyn peninsula off in the distance.

Now I do love beaches and this is a really special one. If you could drop it into the Caribbean Sea – or somewhere equally warm – then it'd be thought of as one of the best beaches in the world and would probably only be close to standing room only as a result. There's actually a beach I know in the Western Cape of South Africa called Vleesbaai which I think is a *doppelgänger* for this beach. But as we're on the south-western edge of a Welsh island, the beach is not busy – in fact, it's amazingly sparsely populated for such a beautiful spot. As I'm here without any of the usual beach paraphernalia, all I can do is tug off my boots and run down to the water's edge – where, sure enough, it is confirmed I'm not in the Caribbean. The iceberg can only just have melted . . .

But no time for chilly toes, I'm nearly at my journey's end and, besides which, there are some people coming towards me. A very smiley man called Geoff approaches, his family gingerly pushing him towards me from behind: 'Do you mind if I have a quick photo with you please, Julia? It's my birthday today.'

'No problem,' I say. 'What a beautiful day.'

Once the pictures are taken, with a grin and wave we leave Geoff and family behind. You can't help but notice the beautiful rocky outcrops all along this beach. They are basaltic pillow-lavas, and they were formed between 500 and 700 million years ago by undersea volcanic eruptions. As the hot molten rock met the cold seawater, a skin was formed which filled with more lava, creating these lovely pillow shapes. It makes for interesting topography around here.

After 8km (5 miles) or so, and near the end of my walk, I've finally reached Llanddwyn Island, home to Wales' patron saint of love – an alternative St Valentine. It's really only an island when it's cut off from the mainland at the highest of tides. Everywhere I turn I'm gasping at the amazing views spread out in front of me: it's so perfect. The same view of the bay that has kept me company for the past few miles is over my left shoulder and out to the right the dark silhouettes of ruins stagger across the skyline. Ahead of me is the church of St Dwynwen, the fifth-century patron saint of lovers. Wales even has its own Valentine's Day, celebrated on 25 January in honour of St Dwynwen, as Graham Williams, the local park warden, tells me, when I meet him by what remains of the building. Graham, as it turns out, is very enthusiastic about all things Welsh.

'St Dwynwen came here either after she rejected the love of a prince named Maelon or after her father, the King, refused to let her marry Maelon. The story goes that she is then attacked by a furious Maelon and Maelon is afterwards turned to ice. She travels to Anglesey where an angel grants her three wishes: she prays that Maelon be released, melted from the ice block, second, that she remain unmarried, and third, that she be forever in service for all lovers in Wales . . . She then retreats here in solitude to live the life of a hermit, until she dies in about AD460.'

'True love doesn't win the day,' I say to Graham. It seems a shame to me that in such a lovely place, her story should be so sad.

'No, indeed. But this church became a significant Catholic shrine during the Middle Ages and this area became an important site of pilgrimage that brought in lots of money for the church, and for the Bangor diocese.' Graham goes on to explain that during the English Reformation the church fell into disrepair, but in the nineteenth century there was a revival of interest in St Dwynwen and people started to come regularly to visit the site.

'Even today?' I wonder.

Oh, yes, Graham reassures me. 'We definitely get our fair share of romantic visitors. Certainly on the 25th of January, cards are exchanged and plenty of couples take a stroll out here.'

There is of course one couple, in particular, of interest to the world whose romantic history is linked with this island. I can see the house they lived in from where I stand: Prince William and his bride, Kate, famously lived on Anglesey, when the Prince was serving as a Search and Rescue pilot at the nearby RAF Valley, flying the yellow helicopters buzzing over us all day. This was the location of their first marital home.

I wonder whether Kate and William came to St Dwynwen's church before they decided to tie the knot . . . and whether or not the relatives dropped in for a cup of tea. I suppose the Anglesey coast is a bit out of their way, but then again his grandmother does own most of it.

It's wonderful to realize that walkers have been coming here for hundreds of years, for no better reason than mine – to enjoy the outdoors and drink in the dazzling landscape. To still be able to see the headland in the distance, with the sun starting to settle around the ruins of the church – you almost can feel the centuries roll back. What a satisfying end it must have been for those weary pilgrims who made the long journey here.

And yet, I've still not reached my final destination. Nearly, but not quite. It's the last few hundred metres of my walk and it looms up in front of me, the gorgeous lighthouse of Twr Mawr (which means 'Big Tower'), which has been protecting ships since the early 1800s. It's only about 10m (35ft) high, but as it stands on a little promontory that gives it a sea height of 24m (82ft), meaning its light reaches 11km (7 miles) out to sea. It may seem odd to find such a sizeable lighthouse on such a small island, but back in the heyday of slate mining, the Menai Strait was full of large ships travelling to and from Anglesey, bearing heavy loads of slate. With the unpredictable waters of the strait to navigate, it made sense to have a lighthouse to warn them of dangerous points on their journey. And it's a fitting conclusion to mine.

Although – somewhere around here someone promised to meet me. Where are they are? And there they are! Ellis, Conor and Liam, with mussels in hand. This really is a beautiful ending to this walk, sitting on the beach at the very end point of the island, eating Shaun's tasty local mussels cooked in a delicious spicy tarragon sauce by Liam earlier. It's certainly the best end-of-walk snack I've ever had.

When we've finished eating, the boys all go skinny-dipping, led by Eric. Four white Liverpudlian bottoms jiggle along the gently lapping shoreline. They must be mad. Actually, I KNOW they're mad: I've dipped my toes in that sea and it's freezing.

And, while the nutters splash about, I clutch my glass of wine and take one last look at the view: Caernarfon Bay, the mouth of the Menai Strait, the mountains of Snowdonia and the Llyn peninsula, all caught in one unforgettable snapshot. This has been a truly magical walk in a place where the mountains meet the sea, where history lives and breathes in the island's nooks and crannies, where new life is always being made, whether it be through baby seahorses or in the form of fabulous cafés. Clearly people have been falling in love with this spot for centuries, from star-crossed lovers and pilgrims to Romans to Royals – and I can see why. Though I didn't find that lovely lost Land Rover, that's somehow soothed by the fact that I do manage to get a photo of the boys skinny-dipping. Something to blackmail them with when they're famous.

WALKER'S GUIDE:
WHERE TO STAY, WHERE TO EAT,
WHAT TO SEE, WHAT TO DO

To eat: Many happy lunches were had at The Marram Grass (White Lodge, Penlon, Newborogh LL61 6KS – https:// curatedby.theoutdoorguide.co.uk/themarramgrasscafe) – so many we ended up interviewing the owners for the show!

To visit: The Sea Zoo Conservation Centre – where they breed baby lobsters and seahorses. Who doesn't like a seahorse? (Brynsiencyn Llanfairpwll LL61 6TQ – http://www.anglesey seazoo.co.uk/conservation-research.html)

To stay: Bodowyr Farm offers beautiful repurposed farm buildings in the area (The Outbuildings, Bodowyr Farm, Llangaffo, Gaerwen LL60 6NH – https://curatedby.theoutdoorguide. co.uk/theoutbuildings): the same owners run similarly good accommodation in the area too, such as Bryn Golau Cottage (https://curatedby.theoutdoorguide.co.uk/theoutbuildings/ brandfront/Menai-Cottages).

To visit: Llanddwyn Island (Ynys Llanddwyn), a place of pilgrimage for lovers in Wales since the Middle ages, reachable from the mainland unless the tide gets very high! (http:// www.anglesey-hidden-gem.com/Llanddwyn-Island.html)

4

THE DALES: THE MALHAM COVE WALK

'The suspense is terrible. I hope it will last'
– Oscar Wilde

'She popped out downstairs next to the fire. I was reading an article about Barbara Hepworth and feeling a tad poorly, but I decided not to wake anyone up and just see what happened.'

I'm at dinner in The Lister Arms in Malham with my friend Amanda Owen, *aka* the Yorkshire Shepherdess, and she's just telling me about the birth of her eighth child, Clemmy, who I'm holding (got to get my baby fix!).

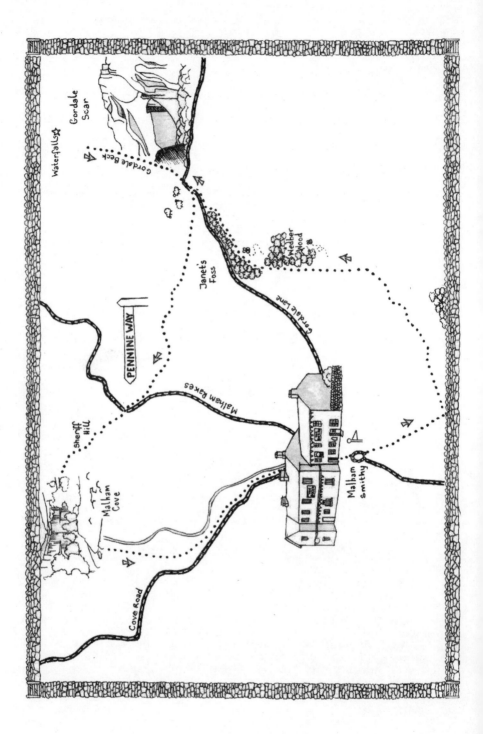

'What did Clive say?' I ask.

'He was quite surprised,' she replies, matter-of-factly.

Clive, Amanda's husband, is used to the catalogue of Amanda's astonishing births. She rarely makes it to the hospital but ends up delivering in a layby or somewhere similar. I met them both ten years ago when I was filming a series about the Coast to Coast walk.

'Do you remember when Clive came to save us that day up on Nine Standards Rigg when I was filming *Coast to Coast*?' I reflect.

'Yes! He came into the kitchen and said "Look wha' I've found at t'moor. Can I keep it?" "Nooooo Clive, I said, you can't!"' she laughs.

Amanda is a fairly extraordinary woman and you can tell why I like her. She and Clive run a 2,000-acre farm deep in the Yorkshire Dales, only about 64km (40 miles) north of Malham, which is why she's popped down to see me here tonight. In addition to running the farm and being a mother, she has also become a bestselling author, a TV 'personality' and a public speaker.

We talk at breakneck speed. Amanda is writing her second book and the rights to her life story have been sold to an American film studio. I can see it clearly – it will be a cracker. The wild children, the beautiful farm, her kitchen full of animals and people and underwear hanging from the drying rack. 'I think Sarah Lancashire or Kate Winslet in your role,' I joke.

'Ha! I'm hoping for *Angelina Jolie*!'

After Amanda leaves, I head for bed – a good rest and I'll be raring to go in the morning.

This next walk finds me in the Dales – a place that couldn't be more different to the bucolic charms of the south-west, the gentle slopes and hidden lanes of Dorset or the rolling hills of the Cotswolds. Dramatic landscapes, deep gorges, waterfalls and winds that on a good day are called 'bracing'. After splashing around on the gorgeous beaches of Anglesey, the landscape will appear rugged and there are plenty of surprises ahead.

I'm starting my walk in the village of Malham, where the hotel is, which makes that start to the day a little easier – right out the front door, that's the kind of walk I like. Malham is one of Britain's most visited villages, although the crowds are not really here for the grey cottages, the quaint village pub or even the sparkling river and packhorse bridge. It's the surrounding area that calls out to tourists, the coach parties, the hikers and families who visit. They're here (as I am) to see the stunning waterfall called Janet's Foss (where the water supposedly has magical powers), the narrow gorge at Gordale Scar and then Malham Cove, a spectacular crescent-shaped cliff carved out of limestone by an ancient waterfall and topped by an lunar-looking limestone pavement. The thousands that come here every year, walking even a part of the Pennine Way to see the high fells, are following in illustrious footsteps: Charles Darwin, writers the Reverend Charles Kingsley (author of the children's classic *The Water Babies*) and J.R.R. Tolkien, and, more recently, the cast and crew of the Harry Potter films – all of them drawn here by the extraordinary beauty of this spot.

I'm pleased to see that, after just over 7km (4.5 miles), I'm due to stop and sample a local speciality, the renowned Malhamdale Pie, which is basically a sturdy local ale and steak pie. After a few hours of trudging along paths and up hills, it's great to have something to look forward to. My friends always joke that I eat like a racehorse.

I'm going on so many amazing walks, it's impossible to say if I have a favourite as each one is special for so many reasons. That said walking in the Dales is always a fabulous experience for me and I'm itching to get started.

Malham is a small village and there have been homes here since the Anglian settlement of the Dales during the seventh and eighth centuries; the village, as we see it today, was established in the seventeenth century, however. In the past, sheep and cattle rearing were the main occupations for people living here. These days, it's mostly tourism that keeps locals employed, though quarrying is still a big industry in the Dales. In addition, there's something that might seem like a blast from the past – a working smithy.

We're going to start on our small section of the 412km (256 miles) Pennine Way by following the Malham Beck. This small stream runs through the village, comes out of the ground near Malham Cove and then runs into the River Aire, south of the village. My walk begins on the packhorse bridge outside the extremely picturesque Lister Arms, the pub in the middle of the village. It's here also that I do my first piece to camera with the bridge in the background:

> The Yorkshire Dales are a mecca for walkers, climbers and cyclists alike and this is a real hot spot. This beautiful Dales countryside is home to spectacular limestone wonders, astonishing dark night skies, the famous Yorkshire Three Peaks Challenge, the highest freshwater lake in England, and of course – *Emmerdale*. And here, in the bustling village of Malham, the great charm of the Dales is brought to life through its landscape, steeped in magic, its long list of Hollywood credentials and scenery so big and bold it can only have been shaped by giants.

Iconic fell walker Alfred Wainwright called Malham Cove the 'greatest natural feature on the whole Pennine Way'. I'd call it one of the greatest natural features in the country.

Before we leave the village, though, I want to show that this part of the country is living and breathing and not preserved in aspic. That people can still see the way of life that used to be so common here and that those living it aren't themselves old – or, like my friend Amanda Owen, born into it. So we head to the smithy to meet a former tax accountant turned village blacksmith, Annabelle Bradley.

Traditional blacksmiths – along with ballers (the person who measure out balls of clay for the potter) and knappers (the person who dress and shape flints) – are a dying breed in this century. And Annabelle certainly does not fit the image of a traditional smithy. She's petite, in her late thirties and has a lovely sunny face and blonde flicky hair. She reminds me a tad of comedian Sarah Millican so if you've got an image of a big burly lass slamming tools around, delete immediately. Married to Nick, a self-employed builder, with whom she has two little girls, Millie and Hatty, Annabelle hopes that they one day may take over the business. It's an interesting thought as Annabelle retrained in her thirties.

'The local church owned the Malham Smithy. [It was] bequeathed to them by renowned blacksmith Bill Wild,' she says, explaining how she got here. 'The church wardens were looking for interested parties to bring life back to the smithy and had hopes that the Malham Smithy would remain just that. A blacksmiths for around 200 years.'

Annabelle and Nick were already living in Malham by that point and the way of life had seduced them.

'We came from a town, where you don't really know your neighbours; [where you'd] come home from work and shut your door and that's it. Here, everyone's involved with everybody; we have a lot of community groups and events where everyone participates.'

So when the opportunity came up to work in the village, it

wasn't a hard choice for her. 'With my children starting school, the two-hour daily commute was beginning to unravel the practicalities of running a family life and a career,' she explains. 'I reached a point where I had to consider rearranging my work life to fit my family.

'Besides,' she smiles, 'Nick and I came here on our first date, so it wasn't a difficult choice. Somebody taught me the basic techniques and then I learned as I went along.'

Being in the heart of the village is a great thing for Annabelle and her family and I can see why, not only does she have a fulfilling job, she's someone who locals can see is working to keep the village alive.

I ask Annabelle what products she makes these days as a blacksmith. 'Is it still horseshoes?'

'Not so much – I get a lot of passing trade. Malham's obviously a very big draw with the walkers, being on the Pennine Way. [There's] lots of local trade as well, I do things for people's houses, the odd tractor repair and quad bike repair, but mainly it's artistic blacksmithing, individual pieces for local people nowadays.'

It certainly hasn't been easy for her. She's found it a tough learning curve, but it's working out well, despite this. 'I get immense satisfaction from spending weeks creating a dramatic sculptural piece, however I have to carefully balance my time to fulfil orders for the more functional pieces for the home and garden.'

It's also something that Annabelle's involved her two young daughters in. 'They do a little bit of forging at the moment. When we go to shows, they make little pieces and sell them. To them, there's nothing abnormal about mum being the village blacksmith.'

I think that's fabulous – *My Mum, the Blacksmith* – what a great children's book that would be. We talk about the past of the village smithy, how it always involved doing a mix of jobs, some crucial to the working of the larger community, such as repairs to vital farm machinery. Although it's not all horseshoes and machine parts as Annabelle proves when she tells me that Bill Wild, the previous blacksmith, had sold one of his pieces to none other than Hollywood legend Bette Davis. It seems she was staying in the village at The Buck Inn, in the early 1950s, while filming *Another Man's Poison*, a Hollywood pot-boiler made immediately after the classic *All About Eve* (one of my favourite films). Unlike its predecessor, it wasn't a successful film, however – in Ms Davis's words: 'We had nothing but script trouble.' But at least she went home happy from Malham, with an original piece of artwork by Bill.

But it's not just Hollywood icons who pop into the smithy in Malham for a spot of shopping. 'I spend a lot more time chatting to the passers by,' she smiles, 'but it's a great way to work – hardly feels like work at all!'

Before I leave, she very kindly gives me a bottle opener that she's made. (Uncanny – how could she know that I could make use of one of those?) I thank her, assure her it'll be put to good (if only occasional . . . honest) use before I set off on my way again.

Back on the riverside path, I bump into a local called Pete who's walking the geese. Yep. Once a week these lovelies get an outing to the river to have a little splash around. It's not quite the same as putting my baby girls in the bath; they're not as noisy or as messy. The geese actually belong to John, the landlord of The Buck Inn, but he's away so Pete has been Goose Sitting. We had geese in Rutland when I was a little girl. Toby and Qwacker used to nip me right on the inside of my leg. Vicious bloody things. Good guard 'dogs' though.

I leave Pete and his friends to get on with their bathing and walk through a kissing gate beside the stone walls and into what just two weeks ago had been a hay meadow. I'm not surprised if you've never seen a hay meadow. There are only about 1,000 hectares of traditional hay meadows left in England today, but some of the best in the country are right here in the Dales. They're a very special environment as they're also home to a wide variety of animals, birds, insects and plants, the latter with such wonderful names as globeflower, great burnet, devil's-bit scabious and oxeye daisies. The wide variety of plants brings in an equally wide variety of bees, butterflies and other insects, making up a good diet for the birds and bats that can be easily seen at different times of day around the meadows. If you're lucky, you might catch sight of hares, rabbits and other mammals racing through the tall grasses. And if it's a warm day – and it isn't today, sadly, as it's October – then anyone standing in a hay meadow would hear the bees buzzing away as they zoom between the flowers.

Here in Malham, the meadows aren't the only habitat for the bees. When I walk into the lush woodland of Janet's Foss, one of the first things I notice is a funny yellow notice as we enter:

'The bee library,' it announces. '12 book nests for solitary bees.'

It's certainly like no library I've ever seen before. At first, I'm pondering what the bee library is, but as I walk through the woods, it starts to make more sense. Hanging from the ash trees, I can just make out some of the titles – *Bee-Keeping for Beginners* and *Beekeeping in Wharfedale*. These books are part of an art and conservation project. Each book is opened out to make a kind of roof and features a nest made with bamboo and wire netting that's been water-proofed and hung up high for solitary bees to find and inhabit. Unlike sociable bumble or honey bees, there are over 200 species of wild solitary bees in England which like to make individual nests – and their numbers are now in steep decline. This project is to help promote their numbers. These are curious little installations – easy for walkers to miss while they're plodding through the woodlands and they're too high up to read, certainly, but what a great idea. If you spot them, you may occasionally see a bee emerge as it heads off to forage again.

Trekking through the woods I feel like I've stepped not just back in time, but *out* of time. I'm walking on a dirt track, with soft mossy ground underneath and the twisted limbs of the trees draped in fronds of green lichen artistically displayed. It's as if the woods are dressed for a film set, they're so perfect. In the spring, the smell of wild garlic fills the wood as the ramsons flower. Locals tell stories of magic here – of Janet, Queen of the fairies, who lives behind the waterfall up ahead, Janet's Foss – 'foss' being the Nordic word for waterfall. It's said that Charles Kingsley drew inspiration for his water-babies and Queen of all fairies from here. For years people have been wedging coins into fallen tree stumps or 'wishing trees', as they pass by on their way to the waterfall. The wavy ripples of coins in the tree trunks look like the spikes of some prehistoric beast. Enchanting waterfalls, intriguing art installations, fairies . . . it's all very dreamy.

And, of course, like Colmer's Hill in Dorset and other places I have been to on these walks, this is somewhere that people also come to photograph, draw and paint. In fact, sitting by the side of the water I come across Katharine Holmes, doing just that. Art is in her blood: her grandmother, Constance Pearson, was a famous Dales artist and Katharine's mother, Philippa, also painted. These women are not unusual: plenty of artists and creative types have been drawn to Malham over the years, including Joan Hassall, the wood engraver, who designed the invitation to Elizabeth II's coronation, who lived here for a large part of her life.

I ask Katharine if she regularly paints outdoors in the area. 'The light is beautiful, filtering through the trees onto the beck,' she tells me. 'I've walked this spot many, many times, but not painted it before.' Her grandmother, Constance, painted outdoors, too, choosing for her subjects the land and the people around here: 'She painted for many years. She was interested in people working the landscape before farming was mechanized. People haymaking, with all the old equipment, herding cattle, that sort of thing.'

I'm interested in hearing more about Katharine's background. 'I seem to be following in the footsteps of my mother and grandmother. My grandmother painted here, the family came just before the Second World War and settled here. Like a lot of people, they came for holidays, and just liked it so much [they] decided to make a home here.

'I also grew up with my mother's paintings in the house and now I'm back in the family home,' she continues. 'A lot of people I grew up with have come back – my neighbour has returned to take on the family farm.' This is a common theme. I've already heard today from others that people born here are returning home. Katharine tells me that her grandmother painted Janet's Foss and that I'll love the place. Katharine's connection to this place reminds me of Marion Taylor, the artist who loves 'her little hill' in Dorset. These landscapes seem to be somehow embedded in these women's souls.

When I get to the waterfall, I can immediately see why

so many people come here to paint. I've been transported to a tropical rainforest. The water cascades down noisily into the pool below, but it's not that high – maybe 3m (10 feet) or so – and it's more picturesque than dramatic. I just want to take my clothes off and dive into the inviting pool below me – except it's a lot colder than the tropics and it's almost winter, so I won't. These ancient falls were formed as Gordale Beck (a stream) plunged over a limestone outcrop into the deep pool beneath; this created a special limestone rock formation, known as tufa, covered in moss – a fragile screen which reaches down to the water below. In recent years, it has been used as a natural sheep dip, with the shepherds wading in up to their chests in the water. I hear strong drink is used to keep out the cold, but I still won't be trying it out for myself, thanks very much – despite being urged on by some of the crew.

'I remember swimming in there on a school trip,' Amanda had told me the night before.

'Wasn't it cold?'

'Nay, you know me, eye don't feel the cold.' In my defence, me Lord, Amanda isn't of Greek descent.

But now I'm going to leave behind the delicate world of the valley and head for the bigger canvas of the gorges and Malham Cove itself. Perhaps it's the variety of the landscape here that led the celebrated American travel writer Bill Bryson, who lived nearby in Kirkby Malham for many years, to refer to the 'serene, cupped majesty' of the area and declare: 'I won't know for sure if Malhamdale is the finest place there is until I have died and seen heaven (assuming they let me at least have a glance), but until that day comes, it will certainly do.'

Well, I certainly respect Bill Bryson's opinion because he's been to so many places on earth, but I guess it depends on what you want and what your family set-up is. Bill writes about people popping into his cottage to borrow eggs and things like that – and recalls one time when he's only in his underpants and hides in his kitchen cupboard while the visitor rummages about. I love coming here – but I'm not sure that I would like to live somewhere where everyone in the village knows my business all the time and makes themselves at home. Not ideal.

I'm walking towards the ominously named Gordale Scar, a ravine and another local limestone wonder. The Scar has inspired many a storyteller and Chris Wildman is a man who knows just about everything there is to know about the tales spun in these parts. Chris is a congenial chappy, who's happy to confirm that, yes, he's been on the Parish Council for nearly seventeen years, seven of those as Chairman and that he's the local butcher, but what he really wants to talk about is sausage – more accurately, chorizo, something not really associated with this part of the world. But not for nothing is Chris known as 'the Chorizo King of Yorkshire'.

Chris chuckles as he tells me about how he earned this name. Farming had become increasingly tough over the years so Chris decided to 'diversify' (the word of the decade in farming speak) into sausages and rapeseed oil. (He also offers butchery courses to those keen to have a go with a machete and a very sharp knife.) His fully cured Yorkshire Chorizo has become a bestseller, and is used in the chorizo flavouring for Pipers crisps. We're discussing his chorizo when he tells me something I really wish he hadn't. I mention that I went through serious salami withdrawal symptoms when I was pregnant as cured meats are off the menu when you're up the duff because of the food poisoning risks. 'Ah,' he says, 'but you're perfectly all right with *fully* cured meat when you're pregnant.'

'Shit. I wish I'd known that at the time – I was having proper cravings.' Ah well, there's always next time, *ha ha*. (If any pregnant mums out there are still a bit uncertain then freeze the meat for four days to kill off parasites, or cook it. Chorizo Pizza – yummy.)

Chris is very active in many aspects of village life, not least in helping with the arrangements that have to be made when film crews want to shoot in the place I'm going to next, Gordale Scar or my ultimate destination, the limestone cliff at the cove. Chris tells me that Gordale is 'spectacular, a fantastic gorge'. Scenes in the BBC drama series *Jonathan Norrell and Mr Strange* were filmed at Gordale, while Steve Coogan and Rob Brydon also filmed parts of the movie *The Trip* at Malham Cove and the surrounding areas.

'You might have spotted your final destination, Malham Cove in the *Deathly Hallows* – where Harry and Hermione

The walks in this book demonstrate Britain's extraordinary range of landscapes, from the gentle coastline of Anglesey (and the largest stepping stones I've ever seen)…

…to the dramatic slopes of High Cup Nick in Cumbria: they call it the Grand Canyon of the Pennines.

The most English of landscapes under a perfect sky: Cleeve Hill in the Cotswolds.

These walks taught me a huge amount about our living heritage: this is Annabelle Bradley's fully functional and entirely traditional smithy in Malham. Sadly not such a nice day!

There's ancient history, too: here I'm standing by the entrance to Belas Knap in the Cotswolds, a Neolithic tomb a good 6,000 years old and still standing.

This is from the first walk in this book, along Dorset's magnificent Jurassic coast. So magnificent I had to sit down for a moment, in fact.

We couldn't have just one coastal walk, though: this is Beachy Head, further along the south coast, an instant natural icon of England.

A pristine dome of blue sky over Kinder Scout in the Peak District: the birthplace of walking in this country and a fitting place for my final walk of the book.

We also ran across plenty of wildlife. Here's a pony failing to appreciate this beautiful view of the South Downs…

…and here is a curious Herdwick sheep in Borrowdale, in the Lake District: a distinctive local breed that still grazes the area in large numbers, thanks to local heroine Beatrix Potter.

Our wonderful crew in Dorset, setting up another perfect shot of a perfect landscape. From left to right, you can see Colin the soundman with his ever-present fluffy microphone, our unflappable cameraman, Jan, and Eric, who (as you can tell from the pointing) directed this episode.

Not a crew member, but even more important: this is me with my dad, Michael, who raised me to love walking and joined me for the Kinder Scout walk.

A path stretching out behind me on the South Downs. I can't remember if I'd just walked it or was just about to, but either way there's nowhere I'd rather be.

take refuge whilst on the run from Lord Voldemort,' Chris tell me, adding, 'they had the biggest camera you've ever seen, but as far as I know not a single member of the cast of crew ever set foot on the limestone pavement. It was all recreated in CGI for the film.'

Although he lived and worked in London for a while, Chris was born here and like many others he returned here to live. He and his wife Jennifer have long since put their roots deep down into the Dales ground – 'although she still calls me an *"offcumden"* – a townie,' he jokes. They have two sons, Oliver and Will who has followed in his father's footsteps. Chris tells me I may bump into Will later in my walk. Before I go, he presents me with one of his chorizo sausages to slip in my backpack. 'Something to snack on later,' he says.

'Thanking you!' I yell as I stride off into the distance, excited now by the prospect of seeing Gordale Scar. I've not just seen it on film and TV. There's also a painting in the Tate Gallery in London, a huge piece of work, about 3m by 4m (12ft by 14ft), by nineteenth-century artist James Ward. He'd been told that no one could paint the majesty and spectacle of Gordale Scar, but this mammoth work, exhibited in 1815, proved everyone else wrong. It's a masterpiece of English Romantic painting, but not all of his contemporaries, Romantic travellers such as the poet William Wordsworth, who came here expecting to be awestruck (and went home happily satisfied), felt the same. The poet Thomas Gray, probably best known for 'Elegy Written in a Country Churchyard', said he could only bear to stay here for a quarter of an hour, but 'not without shuddering', poor bloke. I prefer to recall Wainwright's words about it – 'limestone magic'.

On my way towards Gordale Scar, I can see that the landscape here really has changed dramatically. Gone are the gentle slopes and when I look up at the overhanging rocks, there's a sense of menace. I continue my walk through the field and past the Gordale campsite alongside the Beck before turning the corner into the Scar itself. And, suddenly, it's revealed in all its glory.

Gordale Scar is a 100m (328ft) deep chasm. It's immense: huge blocks of stone tower above us. Everyway I turn, it is the same: large walls of stone with deep lines cut through, like building blocks, with vertical joints and horizontal bedding planes separating them. The over-hanging limestone feels as if it's closing in on us; it really is unsettling. It's not hard to see how its cold and moody rock face has inspired so many stories of sorcery and wizardry. Rumour has it that Tolkien came up with the idea of Helm's Deep, the deep valley and secure refuge which appears in the *The Two Towers*, the second of *The Lord of the Rings* trilogy, while visiting the area.

This great limestone gorge stands at the northern end of the Craven Fault, a 35km (22 miles) geological fault line, running from the borders of Cumbria into the Yorkshire Dales. It was created during the Ice Age when torrents of glacial melt walter carved a cavern that eventually collapsed, somewhere between fifteen and sixteen million years ago, to create a giant limestone gorge and waterfall. Standing looking at it is an assault on the senses: I start to make out faces and weird shapes in the rock face. Perhaps its spell is working on me already.

It's definitely what I'd call bleak, but not in a bad way, if that makes sense. The wind whistles loudly through the gulch and, when we arrive, there are plenty of people climbing up the tricky rock scramble to get to the top of a mini waterfall, some with their dogs in tow. Jan told us that the last time he'd been here, he'd made the climb in icy conditions, with a dog and a camera. I can easily picture it. There's a small scrabble up the relatively drier left-hand side of the waterfall, but in wet weather the water of Malham Beck comes down in a proper torrent and it would be near impossible to clamber up – although certainly more spectacular to look at. One guide that I read said of the climb, 'the rocks can be slippery and you do so at your own risk'. Noted – today is not the day. We still have too much filming to get through.

Peregrine falcons make the Scar their home, but this time we're not lucky enough to see any. I've done a fair bit of bird watching in my time, but I particularly like peregrine falcons because the female is larger than the male and that appeals to the feminist in me. I've always called them 'cheetahs in the sky' even though they actually fly three times faster than cheetahs can run. Peregrines have recorded speeds of 320km

(200 miles) per hour – they're the fastest birds on the planet. I've been lucky enough to see them many times over the years while filming and it's always mesmerising watching a bird of prey in action. They're also one of the great success stories of British wildlife – the population crashed in the 1960s due to the impact of pesticides, but now numbers are back up and it's estimated that there are about 1,300 breeding pairs in the UK. It hasn't been easy for that to happen, not least because there are people determined to steal the peregrines' eggs and sell them illegally.

This is something that I'm in despair about – the serious poaching that is still going on around the world. Before budget air travel, getting to see an exotic or unusual bird or animal was the preserve of the privileged few. These days the world is much more accessible and seeing a beautiful wild creature in its natural habitat is such a thrill. The vile people who trophy hunt endangered animals and hang them on their walls in a secret vault or trade their horns or tusks make me sick. You don't have to go to a far-flung land to see such beauty: we have some pretty amazing wildlife in this country, like the peregrines, which we must take care of. Over the years, nearly 200,000 people have flocked to see them breeding at Malham Cove, where they've been nesting since 2003. So, hands off the eggs, shitheads!

Peregrines apart, the beauty and lushness of this landscape pulls you in, only to shock you with the high drama of the huge and overpowering limestone monolith. And by the time we're finished marvelling and filming it, I'm in need of some fuel, something that local Carol Newhouse rather cleverly knows. That's exactly why she runs a tea van pretty much all-year-round just outside the Scar, open even on Boxing Day.

'I'm so pleased you're here,' I tell her. 'It must be freezing on Boxing Day though.'

Oh, it is, she agrees: 'The cold is the worst bit of the job, otherwise I love it.'

Carol hands me a welcoming cup of hot tea. What bliss!

Carol's husband is a farmer – and he's right behind the van with his sheep, as we drink our tea. Carol grew up in and around Malham, so she's seen a lot over the years – not only the thousands of tourists who come every summer, but also the walkers, the artists and the film crews. She tells me some of the things she's seen from the comfort of her maroon vehicle. Clive Hornby, who was on *Emmerdale* for twenty-eight years, once pitched his tent in the site behind her, but 'almost forgot to pay, I think,' she tells me, smiling.

I finish my tea. It's been a welcome break but I have to be on my way. I've still got to make it to Malham Cove before I can sit down and relax for the day. So off I go again, this time heading upwards, towards open ground. As you gain height, you can't help but notice the criss-crossing grey-white ribbons of drystone walls winding their way across the Dales. With the quarrying industry dating back hundreds of years here, stone from local pits was used to help create these walls and divide up the land. With more than 8,000km (5,000 miles) of them, the Yorkshire Dales' dry stone walls are at the heart of what makes the Dales landscape so distinctive. One of the oldest manmade features in this landscape, the walls are built without mortar or cement. Instead, rocks are pieced together like a jigsaw. It takes years to hone the craft, as a well-built wall should last at least one hundred years, with almost no need to repair it. And, thanks to people like Will, the Chorizo King of Yorkshire's son, it looks like it's a tradition that's being kept very much alive and well today.

Will, a fair-haired, good-looking lad of nineteen is working intently on a drystone wall as I approach him, placing the stones carefully and confidentially in place. His cheeks have that rosy red flush that comes from working outside for hours on end. Will's a passionate young farmer who has things to say.

'It's not like it was,' he says to me. 'We really believe in farming our own land – we just need people to back British farmers for the future of farming in this country.' He explains why the walls are so important, that they're a farming tradition.

'They've always helped keep the sheep where they need to be – [it] makes [our] life a lot easier, especially up on the hills here. Before the sheep, it's thought they were even used to deter wolves.'

'You're about two decades too young to be doing this, Will,' I comment.

'No,' he disagrees. 'Some might think so, but there's a lot of young wallers around here. With a few friends, we do our bit for a few local farmers.'

'It's in your blood, I suppose?' I say.

He laughs. 'My granddad loves a bit of walling.'

I ask him how hard the job is and whether anyone can do it.

'It takes a keen eye, is all,' he says. 'It's about knowing what stone will go where first time around, it doesn't take years to learn. Building them is very much like piecing together a 3D puzzle. It's also hard work, a six-metre section needs about twelve tonnes of stone, all lifted by hand.'

He explains what the process involves. 'A good drystone waller never picks up a piece of stone twice but is able to look at a pile of walling stone and pick up the right size and shape of stone every time.' The wall's strength comes from a number of factors, he tells me: 'Width, keeping a good course, and lots of throughs – a long, reasonably flat stone that holds the wall together. Round here, there isn't many throughs, that's why there's a lot of gaps.'

I ask him if he enjoys it. This seems bleak work, lifting heavy stones in the cold. 'As long as you've got a radio or somebody to talk to, there's no better job, really,' he says simply.

He's kind enough to let me have a go at placing a stone or two – and kinder still when he says that what I've done is fine.

'I'd better go before the wall tumbles down now that I've

touched it. Kiss of death!' I say and thank him before continuing on.

I pass a stark looking stone-built barn called Cawden Flats Barn as I approach the comically named Sheriff Hill – I half expect Deputy Dawg to appear over the hill. I look down at the rolling Dales and the criss-cross pattern of drystone walls that stretch as far as I can see. I wonder how many of those Will or his grandfather have built? From where I stand, I can see a tiny patch of greenery in the distance that is Janet's Foss. It seems a long way off.

I've reached the highest point on our walk now – the top of Sheriff Hill. 'Howdy partner,' I call out to no one in particular. The views really open up. And there it is – the first real glimpse of our star. Malham Cove is nothing short of amazing, a huge sweep of greyish-white cliff. I can remember the first time I saw it, it seemed like something you might only see on a cinema screen, a Western epic. I'd certainly never expected to see anything like this in England – Colorado or Arizona, perhaps, but not here, not in the Dales.

The cove has the appearance of a great abyss – the writer Charles Kingsley once described it as 'that awful cliff' in his novel *The Water Babies*. But it's not awful, unless he meant 'awe-ful' – because I defy anybody to think it's less than awe-inspiring.

There are a couple of ways to reach the plateau on top of the cove. We can either climb directly up the 79m (260ft) high sheer rock face, highlining over 300m (1,000ft) across the open cove (in all weathers . . .) – something that I've seen my friend Tim Emmett do (he *is* a world class rock climber) – or we could take the traditional walkers' trail.

I know which way I'm going.

Increasingly worn by the thousands of boots walking along it each year, this seemingly lunar landscape was created by weathering and ice. Approximately 15,000 years ago, this whole area was covered with ice sheets and glaciers, before the ice stripped away the soil above the limestone, exposing the weak rock to the elements. This colossal crescent-shaped cliff formed then, as melt water, largely from Malham Tarn, carved out the cove as it fell over the edge of the sheer rock face as a waterfall. What a sight that must have been.

Water seeped into the fractures and dissolved the cracks, creating great gaps in between, so creating the ready-made pavement flagstones we see today; the river disappeared underground, when the Ice Age retreated and the climate warmed up, leaving the dry valley we see today. Geologists and geographers the world over will tell you that it is a textbook example of limestone pavement. Here comes the science bit, as that stupid advert told us: understanding the processes by which limestone responds to the environment is key to understanding what goes on at Malham and the Yorkshire Dales, in general. Karst topography is a landscape formed from the dissolution of soluble rocks like limestone. Due to the chemical properties of limestone, which is essentially calcium carbonate, rainwater readily dissolves the rock; sinkholes mark the areas where the surface water disappears underground, leaving the valley dry and creating this spectacular vision. As soils don't form easily on soluble limestone, the rock, scree slopes, crags and pavements that are abundant around Malham are typically bare of plants, apart from in the cracks or grykes. The slabs themselves are 'clints'. It's all very sexy.

To me, crossing the cove is like waking over a giant jigsaw. Jumping from slab to slab, I feel like I am inside a giant Super Mario video game, jumping from one level to the next. You can see how it was suited to the wizarding world of Mr Potter.

I drop down to my knees to peer into some grykes. These sheltered shady conditions are perfect for ferns like hart's-tongue, brittle bladder-fern and spleenwort. You wouldn't expect things to grow in these dark, shaded fissures, where the rocks have split apart in the pavement, but these are a unique wildlife habitat for rare plants and flowers. There is, believe it or not, a different microclimate in the grykes that is more humid and slightly warmer than on the pavement itself, resulting in a different range of vegetation. It's blustery up here on the top of the pavement but down there . . . dog's mercury, lily of the valley, angular Solomon's seal, banberry and enchanter's nightshade all live happily together.

I am trying to sum up the miracle of Malham Cove for the

camera, while also trying to remember not to swear as I do so, but it is all so *bloody* overwhelming. With the mind-blowing views behind me, rumpled fields dotted with small farm buildings far below us, while I look at the camera, I say:

> Just look at those views across the Dales. This is a real wonder of Britain – a 260-foot-high natural amphitheatre and a former giant waterfall – a mini Niagara Falls if you will – no wonder Hollywood comes here. The scale and the drama of this natural amphitheatre is so impressive. In the same way that you'd marvel at the engineering of a brilliant building, you can't help but be amazed by Mother Nature.

But, in the Twittersphere I can be a bit more frank:

'*Holy shit Malham Cove is amazing #awesome #epic #mothernature.*'

That won't win me a Man Booker for literature, but it's from the heart and it's my instant reaction as soon as I clap eyes on this beauty again. And that message got retweeted hundreds of times with so many positive comments from people.

Alison Ayris: *@juliabradbury I remember going there on a school trip back in the 70's – amazing beautiful*

Steven Jackson: *@juliabradbury Nowt better than Yorkshire countryside*

Helenscake: *@juliabradbury beautiful days walking there today #30th wedding anniversary #cheesebutties*

And my favourite, from John Smallman: *@juliabradbury wow! I didn't know you swear! That shit hot that Julia x*

I feel lucky to have grown up in a country that's blessed with so many natural wonders, ones that I'm currently experiencing, some for the first time, others much-loved spots that have personal resonance. A lot of us are proud and a little bit in love with particular areas of our country – a favourite river, a favourite mountain, a favourite valley – and that's something that millions of people share. And as I stare at the landscape before me, I think how brilliant it is that on such a crowded and comparatively small island it's possible to still escape to somewhere as amazing.

Back down in the village, I treat myself to a well-earned pint at The Buck Inn and – a local delicacy – the aforementioned Malhamdale Pie, made with local beef from Malham Moor. I think again about how lucky I am to be doing what I'm doing and, although I'm sure she didn't eat anything as uncouth as a pie when she was filming here, I think about something Bette Davis once said: 'To fulfil a dream, to be given the chance to create, is the meat and potatoes of life. The money is the gravy.'

I shut my eyes tightly, remembering the view from Malham Cove. To walk and explore, to adventure across beautiful landscapes on foot – that's the meat and potatoes. The view? Well, that's the gravy, isn't it?

WALKER'S GUIDE:
WHERE TO STAY, WHERE TO EAT,
WHAT TO SEE, WHAT TO DO

To finish: The Buck Inn (Malham, Skipton BD23 4DA – https://curatedby.theoutdoorguide.co.uk/thebuckinn) will do you an outstanding pie and a pint at the end of a long walk.

To visit: Janet's Foss and the Bee Boles – a natural wonder *and* an art conservation project to encourage solitary bees through nests made of books hanging in trees. You've got to love England (http://www.the-bee-bole.com/2014/07/malham-bee-library_16.html).

To stay: The River House (Malham BD23 4DA – https://curated by.theoutdoorguide.co.uk/riverhousemalham) is an excellent B&B in Malham: for larger groups, Hill Top Farm is good too (https://curatedby.theoutdoorguide.co.uk/hilltopfarm).

To see: Gordale Scar, a beautiful gorge and natural wonder and a popular filming spot, as well as a haunt of the Hollywood stars of their age: the Romantic poets (http://www.malham-dale.com/gordalescar.html).

5

THE LAKES:
THE BORROWDALE
VALLEY WALK

*'The world is a book and those who do not travel read
only one page' – Saint Augustine*

You meet all sorts in the country. There is no 'type', at least not that I've ever come across and I've been looking, believe me. There are people in the finest gear available and there are others with string holding up their jeans; and yet they'll all pretty much feel the same way about fields or gates, duck ponds or a great view – just not about their attire. There are people who live and work in the country, who fiercely cherish their

relationship with it; and there are weekend visitors, out for a stroll and some fresh air – but they'll probably all be able to chat happily together about what they enjoy – the countryside. The chances are that any visitor to the Lake District, where this walk takes place, will meet every single 'type' there is while he or she's walking here. I know I do. The chatty, the silent, the cheerful, the morose – they're all there.

I know this part of the country well as I've spent a lot of time walking here. This is the very spot where my career took a real change of direction. After the first *Wainwright Walks* series was broadcast on the BBC, I suddenly became known as 'that outdoor woman' or the 'walking man's crumpet', according to one paper. Despite the fact that I'd been making all sorts of other programmes for years (I was actually presenting the BBC1 consumer show *Watchdog* at the time), it was the walks that really resonated with audiences and they still do. I get letters from all over the world about them. A publicist once produced a press release about those early walking series with the heading 'The Lady of the Lakes'. I laughed out loud because it conjures up an image of an Arthurian damsel, which is about as far removed from me as you can get: I'm more vintage Lara Croft meets Nora Batty!

Despite having a fair collection of programmes tucked in my girdle, I can pretty much walk around the area of London I live in with no one batting an eye: I'm just another Londoner here. Besides which, there are far more famous people living in my neighbourhood from Ruby Wax to Paloma Faith. Up in Cumbria the story's different. Because of one pipe-smoking Mr Alfred Wainwright (more on him later), I am stopped, asked for photos and questioned, ('Do you really walk the whole way when you're doing one of your programmes?' is one of my favourites . . .), every few hundred yards. I don't know how the Pope does it. It's exhausting. Don't get me wrong. I am always happy to say hello, take a selfie, sign a body part, but the irony doesn't escape me: here I am heading to the hills to make programmes about the beauty and tranquillity of the countryside and it's the one place where I get recognized the most. 'Ooo hello! I was just saying to my husband, wouldn't it be funny if we bumped into Julia, and here you are! Can we have a picture?'

No seasoned British walker could possibly put forward a selection of walks without including at least one featuring the unique landscape of Cumbria's Lake District. Maybe I should scratch the word 'British' from that sentence, because the Lake District receives a staggering 16.5 million visitors every year and many of those are from overseas, drawn to the area by the magic of the Lakes. A ridiculous number of artists, painters, poets and writers have, over the centuries, set up home there, showering us with their creative offerings.

The drive to get there, though, is always torturous so this time my big sister, Gina, and I decide to make things much worse by having a full-blown argument in the car.

'STOP THE CAR!' Gina yells at the top of her voice.

'We. Are. On. The. Motorway! Don't be so bloody stupid!' I scream back.

'STOP THE CAR!'

'YOU'RE RIDICULOUS. WHERE DO YOU THINK YOU'RE GOING TO GO?!!'

'STOP THE CAR!'.

'NOOOOOOOOOO!'

I'm driving so it's a rare moment of me being in control. You see, Gina runs my life, looks after me, tells me where to go and generally keeps me on the straight and narrow. Generally. Now that I have three children and masquerade as a 'responsible person', occasionally our Big Sister–Little Sister lines get blurred. But we love each other unconditionally and incidents like this are soon over.

'I *really* fancy a chocolate Hobnob,' I say.

'And a cappuccino, ' Gina adds.

'I'll leave you at the petrol station then, hey? Ha ha. God I'm funny.'

'You're a pain in the arse is what you are,' she jokes (I think).

Eventually we get past the jams and make it to the edge of the Lakes by early afternoon. It's hard to choose from the many available in this sublime part of the world, but this walk is a dream, an unmissable opportunity to appreciate the wettest and greenest valleys of the Lake District. In just a few hours you can go from being in one of the prettiest hamlets in the region to being at the top of one of Lake District's best-kept secrets, with the most spectacular views across the valley.

The Borrowdale valley itself differs from the rest of the Lake District only in its climate; it rains a lot here – Seathwaite, the village next to Borrowdale itself, is the wettest inhabited place in Britain, with about 3.6m (140in) of rain annually. Keswick, where I've just been, is just over 11km (7 miles) away, beyond the northern shores of Derwentwater; it receives less than half of that amount per year. Because of the rain, the countryside around Borrowdale is particularly green. As one of my many guidebooks archly notes: 'the riverbanks are lush, the valley planted with broad-leaved trees that ration the light, dappling the rocky outcrops and mossy boulders – and if that all sounds suspiciously like a romantic painting, well that's what Borrowdale looks like.' Something of a contrast to the valley's past, when it would have been a hive of activity, with charcoal-burning, mining and even iron smelting industries.

The walk I'm doing isn't arduous, unlike some around the region. There are a few steep climbs and exposed ridges, but this compact 8km (5 miles) walk shows off both the charms and the drama of a landscape that has inspired many poets, writers and artists – from William Wordsworth and Alfred Wainwright to Beatrix Potter and Arthur Ransome – to portray it so beautifully in their work. I'm going to share some of their stories on this walk, as well as some of what I've learned about the Lakes, too, through my love of the area and also my own career.

Before we head off, here's a good pub quiz answer to have up your sleeve: Bassenthwaite Lake is the only official lake in the Lake District. All the others are 'meres' or 'waters', as in Windermere and Crummock Water.

Everything looks as splendid as ever when we get out of the car – and it's great to be back here. This valley was one of Wainwright's favourites: he called it a 'pageant of beauty from end to end'. Just looking up at the crags ahead makes me want to pull on my boots immediately and walk up something grand.

We're kicking things off here in the village of Rosthwaite, with its whitewashed cottages and low-roofed stone barns. It's hard to believe that much around here has ever had an earth-shattering impact upon the whole world; it seems so remote. And yet, not far from where we stand a discovery was made that did just that. In the sixteenth century, a vast deposit of graphite was found in nearby Seathwaite. It remains one of the only known deposits of graphite in this form, anywhere in the world. Locals soon realized that the material was excellent for making marks on their sheep – and so, after graphite's diversion into cannonball manufacture, the pencil industry was born. If you happen to be here when the weather is filthy, head to Keswick to one of the world's most unlikely indoor attractions, the Pencil Museum. As one guidebook says: 'There are only so many things you can say about a stick of lead, but the Pencil Museum tries its best.' I have my own personalized pencil set, thank you very much. Still, I never want to be indoors when

I'm here (except perhaps at night having that classic Cumbrian dish 'Lamb Henry' in one of the trillions of good pubs).

As well as the spectacular scenery, there are plenty of things to be discovered when you're out and about: ferns and lichens on the stones and branches, salmon and otter in the water and abundant birdlife. Whatever you're interested in, as a hardened walker or just someone enjoying the outdoors, you'll find something captivating here. I don't think I've ever heard anyone say anything negative about the Lakes. You know, something like, 'Norfolk is very pretty, but it's a bit flat, Skegness can be pretty in the summer, but the offshore wind farm is atrocious' (I like them), 'Julia is very nice but she can be a bit annoying . . .'

In addition to Rosthwaite being a favourite getaway for Prince Charles and his ladylove Camilla, perhaps more importantly, for walkers, at least, there's a National Trust loo in the car park. It doesn't have a mirror though, which I don't understand as even walkers like to check their teeth before they head off into the wilds.

A small road leads to Yew Tree Farm. The walls marking the boundary of the lane are densely packed drystone barriers made up from local dark stone. At the end of the lane, I stop at the Flock Inn and have a quick chat with Hazel, the owner of the café, a formidable-looking woman with a bonnet of firm auburn hair. Hazel doesn't much like the cameras and she refuses to discuss Prince Charles's occasional visits to the area, but she is happy to talk to me about the hearty local Herdwick sheep, which she calls 'the gardeners of the Lake District', a great and apt description.

That there are so many Herdwicks in the Lakes is down to the efforts of a very famous woman who arguably helped popularize the area with modern audiences. You'll recognize her name – Beatrix Potter, who lived locally. She used the fame that the children's books she wrote, featuring Peter Rabbit and Mrs Tiggy-Winkle, brought her to protect her beloved countryside and to ensure that the hillsides would always have Herdwicks grazing on them. Beatrix bought up fifteen farms and, on her death, in 1943, gifted the land – all 4,000 acres of it – to the National Trust on the proviso that the land was grazed solely by Herdwicks. The sheep themselves are quite distinctive – the purebred lambs are often born predominantly black with white-tipped ears, but as they get older their fleece turns a bluey-grey/light grey and their faces and limbs turn white. They're found grazing at heights of up to over 900m (3,000ft) and are considered the hardiest sheep breed. Their meat, which has a distinctive taste, is much sought after and was even served to the Queen on her coronation in 1953.

As well as a writer and keen walker, Beatrix was an expert breeder of Herdwicks. She was even elected president of the breed's association, shortly before her death, and was the first woman ever to hold the role. I'm a great admirer of a woman making her way in a man's world at a time when it wasn't at all easy to do so. There has, of course, been a surge of interest in Beatrix Potter's life story since the 2006 film about her came out, starring the breathy and, in my opinion, irritating Renée Zellweger.

According to Hazel the only reason that the Lakes are so beautiful is because of the Herdwicks. 'Without them, the hills and mountains around us would be overgrown with bracken and foliage and nobody would be walking anywhere,' she says. That would also mean that she wouldn't sell any of her popular pies. No sheep, no walkers, no café, no village life, no farmers – you can see where this is going. I grab a Herdwick pasty gratefully and move on swiftly. 'You don't want to mess with Hazel,' I think to myself.

'Have a good walk,' she commands. I will!

Joking apart, Hazel is right of, course. These flocks of grazing sheep have helped form the Lake District's distinctive look, but undeniably geology has played its part, as well. The Lakes are divided up into three bands of rocks and this particular place is made up of volcanic rock, formed hundreds of millions of years ago, which thrust upwards to the surface. That's the reason why there are so many crags and outcrops on the fells.

The relationship between the landscape and the life that exists on it is a complex one and it's arguable as to whether we understand it. There's been some debate about the way wolves, reintroduced into Yellowstone, have reshaped the flow of the rivers through the US national park. Through their predation of the deer that were previously running riot there, they have, in turn, impacted on all sorts of life up and down the food chain. In England, however, the last wild wolf was reportedly killed in the fourteenth century not far from here, about 64km (40 miles) south at Humphrey Head, a limestone outcrop. These days if you're keen on the idea of walking with wolves (a bit like the llamas that we met at Sudeley Castle in the Cotswolds, only with bigger teeth) you can walk through the woods of the Lakes with Timber wolves, for a fee, of course. It's not quite back to how things were because these wolves have some Czechoslovakian wolf dog bred into them since it's illegal to let purebred wolves run free in Britain. It does sound like quite an experience though. I did do a dog-sledding husky tour in Switzerland once, but I honestly couldn't get my mind or eyes off all the pooing as we were sledding. You see, when you're sitting in the basket, you're right at *that* level. And they just kept running and pooing and running and pooing and then you sled through it. In the pure white snow. 'This is not very Doctor Zhivago,' I recall thinking. Anyway, I believe that there's talk of reintroducing wolves to the wilds of Scotland – watch this space.

The landscape here is dramatic, with towering hills looming above. The terrain is blanketed with oak and birch woodland and divided by the glistening River Derwent. At one end, a narrow gorge, known as the Jaws of Borrowdale, with Castle Crag above it, which is often described as a 'gob stopper' in the mouth of Borrowdale (remember those old-fashioned, impossibly large round bubble gum sweets?). At the other end, there's

Derwentwater and its magical little islands. Formed at the end of the last Ice Age, the retreating glaciers did us all a favour when they scoured valleys out of the rocks, creating what we say as a typical Lake District view – a deep tarn, wooded slopes and craggy peaks..

You may have seen this view from a different position, sitting in a cinema or at home on your laptop. If you are one of the eighty-eight *million* people who watched the trailer (not the film, just the trailer) on the first *day* of its release for the 2015 *Star Wars* film, *The Force Awakens*, then this landscape may be familiar. There's a scene where the computer-generated fighters whizz across a lake, with green hills ahead of them. Well, that was all filmed here, without the fighters, which were added on later digitally. I wonder if *Stars Wars'* fans will make pilgrimages to Borrowdale in the future to see where their favourite sequences were filmed? Are the Lakes ready for a *Star Wars* convention? It would make quite a picture – hundreds of R2-D2s silhouetted on the top of Castle Crag or Pillar, the mountain to the west.

Meanwhile, back on planet earth, at the edge of the village, I can see the fells ahead of us, Castle Crag in the distance, to my left, while the wooded slopes of the smaller King's How are to my right. The flat valley floor, a pattern of green fields edged with low walls and the occasional tree, sits in the foreground. A perfect view – except now I need to crack on.

In a rare turn of events, we actually filmed the first few

opening sequences in the order they appear on screen. However, I have to interrupt filming to jump in a car and rush to Keswick, where I am rushing to meet up with some members of the charity, Walking with the Wounded. A team of six are part way through a 1,600km (1,000 miles) walk about the country. They are trying to raise awareness and money for wounded service men and women who often are left to fend for themselves following active duty. The plan is to hook up with adventurer Sir Chris Bonington and his son, Rupert, just outside the town and lend our support to the group as they reach town for a warm Lakeland reception.

Despite being in his his eighties, Sir Chris looks incredible, at least a decade younger. He has a tanned healthy-looking face and a strong-looking, wiry body. For someone that has looked death in the face on many occasions, he has kind eyes and a gappy smile that rarely is missing.

I'm totally in awe of him. He's climbed many of the most difficult mountains in the world, often more than once – the Eiger, Annapurna, Everest – and he's still climbing at his advanced age. He summited Everest, having led expeditions there before, when he was fifty; and when you think of it, the advances in equipment and clothing technology over the last twenty to thirty years make those earlier achievements seem even more remarkable. To have that drive, that ambition – and to have the ability to carry it out and see it through to the end – well, as I said, I'm in awe.

I'm startlingly average at most things. I have an enquiring mind, I'm a fast learner and I've always been able to think on my feet. It helps to possess confidence on TV and to be able to communicate with the camera, but I can't spell, I don't understand mathematical equations – or, as my schoolteachers will verify, even easy sums. I don't remember important dates. I can't play a musical instrument or ski brilliantly. I can *half-do* quite a lot of things and I'm game, but I'm not talented in one particular area. Unlike Sir Chris Bonington.

'Perfect timing, Julia!' Rupert, Sir Chris's son, says as we draw up. 'Thanks for coming, now let's get some photos taken.'

After a cheery, 'Hi lads!' and some introductions, I man-oeuvre myself into the middle of the team and grin at the cameras, at the same time stretching my arms out to hold on to the shoulders of the two lads either side of me. Well, I would do if I could stretch my arms around them. They really are walking around Britain. They're carrying massive backpacks, stuffed full of everything they needed to eat, sleep and walk with on their hike.

'How d'you carry all this weight?' I gasp to their laughter. Finally, photos done, we head into the middle of Keswick together.

The last time I was in Market Square in Keswick was back in 2009, when I turned on the Christmas lights with HRH The Prince Of Wales, following the disastrous Cockermouth floods. When I met him earlier that day for a photocall, shaking hands on a bridge, I was just another hand to shake in a long line-up, but by the time we pushed the button together that evening (Me: 'Shall we do this thing?' HRH, in somewhat surprised voice: 'Yes, let's'), he had been fully briefed and had my CV down pat. He even knew how many viewers watched *Countryfile*, the series that I was presenting at the time with the lovely Matt Baker. I subsequently spent a bit of time with Prince Charles because he agreed to be guest editor of the twenty-fifth anniversary programme. I'm one of the few people to have interviewed him several times at his farm, Highgrove, in Gloucestershire, which I did for that episode. I even laid a hedge with him. At one point I was bashing a post into the ground. 'Come on! Give it a good whack,' he encouraged, as I nearly walloped his finger. It would have made good telly, but I'd have probably ended up incarcerated in the Tower of London.

Prince Charles has a great sense of humour and a real twinkle in his eye. He's also got something in common with us, Dear Reader – he loves to walk.

'Walking is very important to me,' he explained. 'Rather like some people need a cigarette, I need a walk. That's where my best thoughts come from.' He almost got his own back during our interview when a stray bit of foliage flicked into my face while we were rooting around on the floor: 'Oh, we don't want to damage expensive BBC property! We'll be in real trouble,' he chuckled.

Prince Charles's views about the countryside are well

informed and he's very passionate about a whole host of issues, but I think it's incredibly difficult to broadcast and come across sincerely when you're a member of one of the most famous aristocratic families in the world. I won't go into our conversations about soil and hedges, but he's not the crackpot who reportedly talks to plants that the media likes to portray. (The jury is still out, BTW, on whether talking to plants actually has an effect, although, in 2007, South Korean scientist Mi-Jeong Jeong claimed playing Beethoven's *Moonlight Sonata* to rice plants encourage faster growth and earlier blossoms. Maybe they were trying to escape that particular piece of music?)

The crowd cheer noisily as the Walking with the Wounded guys make their way towards the square. Along with the Mayor, it seems as if the whole town is on parade, complete with a choir, flags and bunting. Hundreds of people are waving at us as the team heads for the welcoming point. Sir Chris and I hang back, both slightly embarrassed to be sharing their moment.

'I feel a right old cheat tagging along,' I whisper to Sir Chris. He nods in agreement, but we both happily accept the pints of Thwaites Wainwright Golden Ale that are being poured at the finish line. It's too good an opportunity for me to miss and I pull out my phone and ask Sir Chris if he'd mind if I took a selfie with him – although we're interrupted when, unusually, some young lads who can't be more than ten ask for my autograph and a photo. My fan base is usually at least thirty years older.

After I post the photo of me and Sir Chris on social media, my Twitter followers respond to it in their droves, with lots of nice 'wows'. Sometimes, when I'm in the papers or on the telly, people comment about how irritating they find me – and I get it. When you're in the public eye, people form an opinion: not everybody will like you or like who they think you are. Sometimes I get to respond directly and say: 'Yep, I can be really irritating; try living with me.' You can't choose what rubs you up the wrong way, after all. It's when people take it to the next stage and start being abusive that I part company with them. Goodbye you dirty trolls. Be gone. I'm sure Sir Chris Bonington doesn't have such issues though. Not only is he excellent at a lot of things, climbing apart, he's also such a nice bloke so there surely can't be anyone who thinks he's annoying.

The time's come for me to head back to my walk, but the good news is that Sir Chris agrees to meet up with me again later on. I'm looking forward to hearing more from him about climbing in Cumbria and how it compares with some of the truly exquisite places he's visited over the years.

There are probably more sheep here than on Everest, of course. Something that's been part of the life here, long before the walkers and the tourists, before any industrial revolution came and went, is farming. And, as in this region, that means sheep and sheep herding, I am now on the lookout for a shep-herdess named Rosie, who's working on one of the farms ahead of me.

When I come across her, Rosie, a bonnie blonde in her twenties, I'd guess, is calling to her Meg, her Collie, who is guiding a flock of Herdwicks down a lane into a field. It's fascinating not just to watch but also to listen to Rosie, as she stands calmly, arms down by her sides, whistling and shouting calls out, instructing Meg to round up and herd the sheep towards the corner of the field we're now standing in.

'Cum bye. Cum bye . . . there's a good girl . . . walk on. Good lass.' The four-year-old dog expertly harasses and harries the sheep into the right place.

'That's impressive,' I comment.

'Ah Meg's being lazy. She's a bit tired after a long day yesterday. Anyway it's easy to herd the sheep in a field, but get them up on to the fells and it's a different story. They're bad for going into crags,' she tells me, 'and you can't get them out. It's dangerous for your dog to go in, normally you'll go in, but it takes longer to climb up.'

I stare at the sheep, which have been such an integral part of life in the Lakes since the twelfth century – believed, by some, to have been brought over by the Vikings – and can't imagine Rosie struggling to control them.

They're quite handsome. 'They're good to look at,' Rosie agrees. 'Everyone thinks they're the bonniest sheep about.'

Rosie is a local girl. Her mother has a farm 'just over the hill'. She studied agriculture for a year at Newton Rigg, before spending a year working in New Zealand with her sister. Rosie then came back to Borrowdale, while her sister stayed in the 'land of the long white cloud' and married a shepherd – so there must be something in this Borrowdale water.

She knew how hard being a shepherdess would be: not just the prospect of working outdoors, in all weathers, but also that it's not the easiest of professions to get into. I know this from conversations with my friend Amanda Owen (from ITV's *The Dales*) who's a shepherdess. Now the unusual thing about Amanda, who I mentioned earlier, is that she didn't grow up in a farming family, so her choice of work was quite unusual. And as preposterous as it sounds, if you're a woman in this world, it can be really tough. I tell Rosie about the farmer who hired Amanda early on, on the proviso that she couldn't look happy when his wife clapped eyes on her. 'I don't want 'er indoors to see a smile on yer face.' Bloody hell.

Things haven't changed that much. 'I came here and asked Stanley [a local farmer] if he'd take me on,' Rosies says. 'He was a bit wary at first – what with me being a girl – but he said yes. Now he says it was the best thing he's done, so I was quite chuffed.'

Rosie thinks being a woman in this traditionally male world has its advantages though, even if the men can be sceptical about her strength and ability: 'They all think you're just not strong enough, like boys, but at lambing time I think a girl's better because you're slower with the lambing.'

'Do you mean you'll be more compassionate?' I ask.

'A boy would just yank it out, I think,' she explains. 'You know how much pain they're going through!'

I'm encouraged to think Rosie can make a viable living as a freelance shepherdess, but it still surely must be a hard job, striding out into the fields when it's sleeting down and she must have days when she would rather be doing something else. Or perhaps it's the best job in the world?

'Oh, it's nice to work here,' Rosie says. 'I do love the job and wouldn't want to change it for anything. I know it'll be raining for most of the time here [and] you just get on with it. You're outside – I wouldn't want to be stuck inside.'

There is obviously a sense of community between the farmers and Rosie tells me that when Stanley had to have what she calls 'a heart do' and she was in charge of his farm while he was away, the other local farmers helped out, too. That, in turn, helped her as one of the local farmers saw firsthand how hardworking she was and took her and Meg on to manage his own sheep. Rosie undeniably loves Meg, as well as her other dogs, Jess and Pip, and she believes that they love the outdoor life, too, and the job.

'Everyone thinks that they don't, that you make 'em work hard, but they love their job. They wouldn't want to be locked in a kennel or anything like that, really.'

It's hard to argue with that, of course. Most farmers I've talked to about sheepdogs, in my experience, just see them as workers, so it's unusual to meet someone like Rosie, who thinks of them as more than that, recognizing that, just like her, they would hate to be stuck inside.

Rosie's ultimate goal is to run her own farm with her boyfriend ('Who doesn't like sheep!' she laughs), but, as absurd as it may sound, it's not so easy to find one, even in a land as vast as the Lake District. Falling commodity prices, rising overheads and a strong pound are among the factors that make it increasingly hard for small farms to turn a profit. And, if a family has managed to hold on to a farm in this climate, the chances are it isn't going to let it go without a fight. There are, however, plenty of sheep – which goes back to the efforts of Beatrix Potter.

Although her life and books have made Beatrix a household name, she isn't the reason that the Lakes became such a magnet for visitors. They were coming here long before she moved to Cumbria. The 'Grand Tour' was the historical travel phenomenon of aristocratic Europe in the late seventeenth and eighteenth centuries. Considered a rite of passage for upperclass young men before they took up their aristocratic duties, these voyages of discovery are credited with creating a dramatic improvement in British architecture and culture during that time. The French Revolution, which began in 1789, effectively closed off the traditional Grand Tour circuit, resulting in young English nobles travelling closer to home to such beautiful places as the Lakes. In the early nineteenth century, however, railways changed the face of tourism for ever by making it cheaper and far easier for millions in the cities of the industrial north to travel, opening the Lakes – and other places previously inhabited by Britain's elite – to a greater and more socially diverse population.

Anyway, it's time to head off. As I march away, I bump into Rosie's mum. 'Thanks for chatting to her. Keep up all your good work for the countryside,' she says with a big smile.

'I'll do my best,' I grin back.

A little further up the gravelly lane from the farm, I reach some pretty stepping stones, which provide a crossing over the River Derwent. It's a tranquil spot, with gorgeous views out to some vivid green hills. There's a hint of bright blue in the sky today. This is the only day that it hasn't rained for weeks so we're lucky. As I tippy toe over the stones, doing my best not to topple in. I remember The Bowder Stone, further down the valley.

The Bowder Stone is a 2,000-ton rock delicately balanced, standing like a ballet dancer on point on one corner, not on a flat side, at well over 9m (more than 30ft) high and was deposited there during the last Ice Age. You can climb up one side of it, something which makes many people look worried, as if they might topple it by standing on the top, but it's been standing strong for the last several thousand years. I'm not passing it on my walk today, but I love clambering up the ladder and standing on top of something that's perched so precariously. After all, it's not everyday you get to experience standing on an Ice Age boulder, dragged all the way from Scotland. If you fancy having a go up it yourself, you'll find it at grid reference NY25401639. There's even a pay and display car park.

One of the things people miss when they come to the Lakes, because their eyes are lifted to bloody great boulders and extraordinary valleys and beautiful mountains all around them, is what's going on at their feet. Borrowdale, because it's so damp, is a fantastic and unusual habitat for all kinds of bird and insect life and also the plants that they thrive on. As I wander along the riverbank through Johnny Wood (which is an actual oak woodland, not a whiskey), situated on the road here from Rosthwaite to Seatoller, I peer down at the secrets of the floor. The exposed roots of the trees create wiggly pathways to follow.

Whoever comes up with plant names does such a fantastic job. Better than the person who comes up with street names, anyway – plant names are so much more imaginative. And they really have gone bonkers: purple saxifrage, moss campion, alpine *and* shrubby cinquefoil, alpine lady's-mantle, alpine catchfly and, best of all, alpine mouse-ear. Ferns such as the rigid buckler and mosses and lichens and wild flowers cling to the side of the crags around here. There are colourful bog-mosses, cotton grasses and bog asphodels. In the meadows and on the areas at the edge of lanes, there's wood crane's-bill, globeflower, wild angelica, roseroot, rosebay willow herb, knapweed, wild parsnip, sneezewort, yarrow, harebells and the less-pleasant sounding fleabane. Others that you might see by the water's edge are the pinky-white flowers of bog bean along with water-starwort, quillwort and floating bur-reed. On the more marshy areas, bog orchid, sundew and the unlovely named bladderwort can be found.

It's a great list – and these are just a few. There are so many other species. People think of the Lakes as a plain environment of sheep-dappled hillsides and craggy outcrops, but the reality is that we often don't realize how much rare beauty we're walking past or on top of. Look up and you might see ospreys, peregrine falcons (my favourites) or kingfishers; and, scampering in the trees of Johnny Wood itself, you might just catch a glimpse of the red squirrels that are flourishing here in the valley.

I reach the little hamlet of Seatoller, where another gathering of whitewashed cottages awaits me. Nowadays it's set up for tourists and walkers, hiking their way around the area. It's a good spot for some adventurous ghyll scrambling too, which is happening right now, with a group of blokes partaking. 'Ghyll' is a Norse word meaning a 'mountain stream' and ghyll scrambling – or gorge walking – involves ascending and descending a ghyll, of which there are many in the Lakes. This is just one of the outdoor activities that the region has become famous for, attracting millions of tourists from around the world each year.

'All right guys! Looking good,' I call out, but everyone in the team is too engrossed in the wet task at hand to hear me. Sadly, I didn't pack my wetsuit so I can't join them. I move quickly on before they see me and try to tempt me in. Originally Seatoller was built to house workers in the graphite mine and the quarrymen from the slate mines at Honister where I'm going to be going later, but, for now, I continue on, opening a gate alongside the road to head up a fairly steep grassy incline. The valley begins to open up as we climb higher.

It's great to look back and see how lovely the landscape and view is and yet, how strange to think that it was once seen as ugly. In 1724, Daniel Defoe, of *Robinson Crusoe* fame, called the Lakes 'all barren and wild, of no use or advantage either to man or beast', and claimed that they had 'a kind of inhospitable terror in them'. Well, times change and just fifty years later, in 1770, Thomas Gray, the very same poet who 'shuddered' at the sight of Gordale Scar in Malham, raved about this area. In particular, he admired,

> the jaws of Borrowdale, with that turbulent chaos of mountain behind mountain, rolled in confusion; beneath you and stretching far away to the right, the shining purity of the lake reflecting rocks, woods, fields and inverted tops of hills, just ruffled by the breeze, enough to show it is alive.

I stop for a few moments to have a bite of some millionaire's shortbread. I need to keep my energy levels up. I should really be eating some of the locally produced Kendal Mint Cake, but I have an admission to make – I'm not a big fan of it, even though it's walkers' fare. When Sir Edmund Hillary and Sherpa Tensing reached the summit of Everest in 1953, they had Kendal Mint Cake in their backpacks and the packaging later used to proudly proclaim this: 'We sat on the snow and looked at the country far below us . . . we nibbled Kendal Mint Cake.' So if you want to feel like a mountaineer, pack a bar or two. It tastes like extremely minty white sugar cubes, in my opinion. A more recent addition to the stable is a Kendal Mint Cake liqueur which is 24 per cent proof. Now, that's more like it.

Billy Bland, the man I'm about to meet, certainly may have been fuelled by Kendal Mint Cake to do what he's famous for. It's something that's way beyond me and I think I'm pretty fit: fell running, an exhausting activity that involves running at top speed up and down hills. It's often thought to have originated here in the Lakes, where farm labourers and shepherds would take part in informal contests across the fells.

One of the most famous fell runners, Billy is a ten-time winner of the Borrowdale Fell Race, a 23km (17 miles) run that climbs up to over 2,100m (some 7,000ft). He holds the record for completing the race in two hours, thirty-four minutes and thirty-eight seconds. He is also the record holder for the Bob Graham Round, an 8,299m (27,000ft) ascent of more than 42 of the highest peaks in the English Lake District. Billy achieved this in just thirteen hours and fifty-three minutes!

Billy has pure white hair and is as thin as a whippet (as you'd expect for a long-distance runner). He's a frighteningly fit 68 and was born here in 1947 when this valley was far more remote than it is today. 'We didn't have electrics till about 1960, so there wasn't a lot to do,' he comments in his thick Lakes accent. The valley was everything and it was his playground.

Both his father and uncle were farmers and the children were supposed to keep out of their way. With two brothers and sister, life was competitive and Billy and his siblings were always challenging each other. Wherever they went in the valley, the brothers would try to outdo each other, running up and down the hills.

'I wasn't the best,' says Billy, then he adds wryly, 'but achieved more than t'other two.'

I ask him what the secret to his success is as he still holds a number of records.

'A lot of training. I never considered myself good, so my options were limited – to train harder than them. I was very fortunate that I was good at downhill, probably to do with my breathing, as much as anything; my two brothers were good at downhill too. Never entered your head you were going to fall – occasionally you did, but never entered your head you would.' And it's this sure-footedness that gave Billy an advantage, right from the start: 'When I first started, couldn't keep up to get to top, but I always knew I would have a fair chance coming down.'

But his big secret is sleep. 'Before a race I'd go t'bed about seven o'clock and get a good twelve, thirteen hours in,' he says.

Twelve or thirteen hours? That's a coma, not a sleep! God, what I would do for thirteen hours' sleep as a mother of three.

Billy's catchphrase, which punctuates our conversation, is, 'Well, whatever'. He uses it to indicate his indifference to any fame his achievements have brought him. 'People make a big fuss, you can't do nowt about that, can you. Well, whatever.'

He stopped running a few years ago: 'I ran a race when I was fifty. It was only a local show, but I ended up winning it, although I shouldn't have. But the fire was going out, and I started pulling muscles when coming off the building site. Well, whatever.'

On the building site though, people were talking about cycling and the coast-to coast challenge. Billy thought he'd give that a try. 'I bought a £500 bike [and] thought that was it, but I love my cycling now and have a £3k bike.'

I wonder what it is that motivates Billy to push himself like that. 'I get the same fix out of it I got out of my running. There's some drug there involved. I don't know what it is,' he muses, 'but the body produces something – I'd be a grumpy old sod if I didn't get it on my daily exercise!'

Living in London or any big city or town, you can forget that the pace of life is very different when you're a country dweller. Talking to Billy, I'm conscious that he is very much in tune with himself and life in the valley, but probably doesn't like the modern world much. He confirms this, saying that he came from 'a completely different era' and that now he sees people carrying about mobile phones and tablets and 'and all that crap', he thinks that they 'barely have enough time to talk to one another'.

'You don't have a mobile?' I enquire. Once upon a time he did have one it turns out, but he never used it so the network provider switched it off.

He shrugs, saying, 'Makes life more complicated. I'm a simple person who likes to live a simple life.'

Billy is a real character. Proper old school and a great advert for leading an active outdoor life. When I tell people who are into their long-distance running that I've met Billy they're always a bit star struck. He's a hero in these circles. But I think I'll just carry on with the walking, thank you very much!

'Right, I'm ganna yam. Hello to the la'al uns.' Billy turns to walk away (translation: 'Right I'm going home. Say hello to the little ones').

'See you Billy. Thanks for the chat,' I say taking my leave of him.

As I carry on up the path I come across a reminder of an old friend. A signpost for the coast-to-coast trail, the path made famous by my friend Alfred Wainwright. I've walked that tough route, over 300km (about 190 miles) from the Irish

Sea, in the west, to the North Sea on the east coast. Luckily, my walk today's a little shorter, but it is still a great place to be reminded of Wainwright's achievements and it's a special place in the heart of walkers throughout the country.

Wainwright really did inspire a love of walking in people, not just me, but hundreds of thousands, probably millions, of people. It was his way of presenting what he loved about a place that made him so special. His hand-drawn pictures of the fells in his pictorial guides to the Lakes are something that anyone familiar with Wainwright will mention. I'm proud to be a member of the Wainwright Society because his legacy – his books and through them his love of the Lake District – not only brings the fells and the tarns to life, but also introduces new visitors to the Lakes every year.

I wander along the old quarry road and it's not long before I catch my first glimpse of Castle Crag, which, from this perspective, looks like it's still some distance away, although, in reality, it's not. It's just the way the path winds. It's fascinating to think that this track was once regularly used by the quarrymen and the miners who would have walked up here every day to come to work and that what we today think of as a place of gentle recreation, a trail into the hills, was for them their daily commuter route. They weren't heading, in rain or shine, to the outdoors, but down into the quarries or deep into the ground. There are mounds and caves dotted all around the fells.

I'm taking a little diversion here, however. You see I can't come this close to Honister Pass and not visit the Honister Slate Mine, even though it's not technically on the walking route. I pull on a safety helmet and greet a friendly guy called Roly at the mouth of the mine. Of course, the first thing I notice when I'm inside is that there's slate literally *everywhere*. I'm engulfed in it. Roly explains that this is because we're in the middle of a slate seam. 'You're inside a volcanic sandwich,' he comments, which is probably the best geological description I've ever heard. Above my head is a large slab of lava and we're in what Roly calls 'metamorphic volcanic ash'.

The other reason for this detour is that I have a personal attachment to this slate and this place. I have filmed here many times before and the owner of the mine, Mark Weir and his partner Jan Wilkinson, are friends of mine. When I needed to get to the Lakes in a hurry to turn on the Christmas lights in Keswick with HRH The Prince of Wales, Mark phoned me up and asked if I wanted a lift.

'That would be amazing if you're sure?' I said.

'Yep, no problem. I'll meet you at Elstree aerodrome about 10 o'clock,' he replied in his thick Lakes accent. Mark wasn't coming to pick me up in his Landy, you see, which would have been good enough as I've already said I've got a soft spot for these vehicles. Instead, he was coming in his Gazelle helicopter. Great fun.

Regretably, Mark is dead now. He was killed tragically in a helicopter crash on 8 March 2011 aged just forty-five.

He called Jan to tell her he was on his way home after a day working at the mine and just never made it. We were all devastated when we heard the news. When a friend dies, the impact is deep and raw. I vividly remember Gina, my sister, calling me in floods of tears. I told her to slow down because I couldn't understand what she was saying. I can't even imagine how Jan felt when she realized what had happened. Mark and Jan have three wonderful kids together: Prentice, who's eighteen, Pierce, who's sixteen and gorgeous Georgie Blue, who's fourteen (going on forty). The boys look so much like him it's crazy. Flying was Mark's passion and I can honestly say I didn't see him passing away quietly in a chair at the age of ninety, as he was daring, courageous and fun. Still, he left us far too soon.

Mark's obituary of 8 April 2011 in the *Guardian* newspaper states that he was 'an exuberant businessman who brought new life to the ancient slate mines of the English Lake District. Restless and brimming with ideas, in 2006 he installed the UK's first *via ferrata*, or mountain climbing ladder, high in the fells; and was working on plans for a zip line and an underground theatre at the time of his death.' He did a lot for the area.

So, my visits to Honister, 'the last working slate mine in England', are now always tinged with sadness. Still, as Roly runs through the list of buildings and locations where the slate has been used, I have cause to smile.

'The Ritz Hotel, parts of St Paul's Cathedral, as well as

Buckingham Palace and huge swathes of Regent Street,' he says proudly.

'And my bathroom,' I add.

I'm not much good underground so after a couple of hours in the mine, I'm happy to get back outside. In the sunshine, once my eyes have adjusted to the light, I stride on to my next stop, the tranquil stream of Tongue Gill. I'm less than a kilometre away from Castle Crag now and the light is just beginning to dim. This place is so calming, the sound of the water just transports you away from everything into a peaceful happy place. For me, it's the perfect spot from which to absorb the beauty of this valley. It fills me with awe. I am, of course, far from the first person to feel moved and inspired by the valley. Famously, the poet William Wordsworth, who lived and worked in the Lakes, published the *Guide to the Lakes* in 1810 (it was reissued with updates, in 1822). Now you ask almost anyone to recite a line about nature from a poem and they'll probably trot out, 'I wandered lonely as a cloud', which Wordsworth wrote about daffodils almost 30km (18 miles) to the east of here, in Ullswater.

I decide to tell the tiring crew a joke: 'Back in the 70s I went into the hairdressers at Alnwick in Northumberland and asked for a perm. The hairdresser said, "I wandered lonely as a cloud . . ."'

Nothing. Not a smirk. Thanks guys.

But it's not William Wordsworth that interests me: it's his sister.

Dorothy Wordsworth lived with William, even after he was married, and her writing – in prose, often in the form of letters – was to form the basis of a lot of her brother's work. In the revised 1822 edition of *Guide to the Lakes*, William quotes extensively from a letter of Dorothy's, although he only credits her as 'a friend'. Dorothy's writing about an ascent of nearby 'Scaw Fell' that she undertook with a female companion, a maid, a 'man to carry our provisions' with a 'statesman shepherd of the vale' as a guide. In the letter, which William turns into a definitive account of climbing 'Scaw Fell', Dorothy begins by writing about their starting point:

> And we all dined together in the romantic Vale of Borrow-dale, at the house of a female friend, an unmarried lady, who, bewitched with the charms of the rocks, and streams, and mountains of that secluded spot, has there built herself a house, and though she is admirably fitted for society, and has as much enjoyment when surrounded by her friends as anyone *can* have, her cheerfulness has never flagged, though she has lived more than the year round alone in Borrowdale, at six miles distance from Keswick, with bad roads between.

When they reached their destination, she sets the scene beautifully:

Not a blade of grass was to be seen – hardly a cushion of moss, and that was parched and brown; and only growing rarely between huge blocks and stones which cover the summit and lie in heaps all round to a great distance, like skeletons or bones of the earth not wanted at the creation, and there left to be covered with never-dying lichens, which the clouds and dews nourish; and adorn with colours of the most vivid and exquisite beauty, and endless in variety. No gems or flowers can surpass in colouring the beauty of some of these masses of stone which no human eye beholds, except the shepherd led thither by chance or traveller by curiosity; and how seldom must this happen!

When I look about me now, it certainly seems far greener than the place where Dorothy ends up, but the stark beauty of the Lakes is brilliantly captured in her words and I'm now looking forward even more now to reaching the top of Castle Crag, 'the bones of the earth not wanted', and having the land below laid out in just the way Dorothy Wordsworth describes.

Dorothy's not the only person who saw this place as somewhere way, way off the beaten track. In the early 1900s, a man called Millican Dalton (the self-proclaimed 'Professor of Adventure') turned his back on civilization and moved into a disused split-level quarried cave, Dalton's Cave, which is carved out of the side of eastern side of Castle Crag. (You can have a look inside on your way down from the fell.) He lived here during the summers for the next forty years (originally he spent winters further south, living in a tent in Buckinghamshire but he gave that up eventually). He made his own clothes and camping items, but he did make one concession to the modern world – he would walk down to Keswick to buy his coffee. He worked as a guide and climber to earn money, offering all sorts of adventures to men and women who came to the Lakes – and among those advertised in 1913 was 'Exploration of a Cave', 'A Thunderstorm in the Mountains (weather permitting)', 'Dangling over the Precipice' and 'Varied Hairbreadth Escapes'. These were real adventures and, by all accounts, time spent with Millican was fun, intrepid and entertaining. If you peek into his cave, you can still see, carved on the walls, his motto: *'Don't waste words, jump to conclusions.'* Quite.

As I head up to the place where I'm rendezvousing with Sir Chris Bonington, a stray lamb bounces in front of me and then runs along a precariously narrow ledge, dead-ending itself in a panic and nearly toppling over the edge. At the last moment, it rights itself, proving exactly what shepherdess Rosie had said earlier about the Herdwicks being a tricky breed of sheep to steer on the fells. They're more like mountain goats, but they're not quite as dextrous as they think they are.

'Afternoon, little lady,' I call out to her. I've decided it must be a 'she'.

Sir Chris is waiting for me. He tells me that he's very pleased to be here, as Castle Crag is his 'favourite summit', which is saying quite something when you consider all the places he's been to and the mountains he's climbed. I ask him jokily, which one's better for a climber, Castle Crag or Everest, the tallest mountain in the world?

'You can't compare them,' he says. 'They're both fantastic in their own different ways. Castle Crag's a whole sight more fun! There's some good rock climbing up there – and it's scary, too. All this rock is all slate. It's slippery; it's unreliable. Even when I was climbing at the heights of my powers, going thirty years back, I was turned back once or twice on Castle Crag.'

Wow – to think I've climbed somewhere Sir Chris Bonington describes as 'scary'. Brownie points.

Sir Chris is a local. I ask him how long he's lived here.

'I moved to the Lakes in 1963,' he tells me. 'I had no money whatsoever. I'd made a bit of money climbing the north wall of the Eiger [but] most of that went to buying a mini van. We got 110,000 miles out of it.'

Over fifty years in this lovely place, I think, lucky man. 'You've already told me Castle Crag holds its own against Everest – but what about the rest of the Lakes? To someone who's travelled [to] the world's wild places, is this area truly special?'

'It's an exquisitely beautiful place,' Sir Chris comments. 'In its own way, there's nowhere in the world more beautiful. It's rather like the spokes of a wheel,' he continues, stretching out his fingers to make his point. 'The valleys go out and each valley has its own individual character – the way it's used. There's an extraordinary variety within a very small area.'

Oh, now I'm itching to get to the top of Castle Crag and to see the tapestry of fields, hedges, woods and lakes sprawled out before us. I wonder if it still thrills Sir Chris as much now as it did when he first climbed it, over fifty years ago. He's very clear on that: 'That view we're going to get is magic, one of the best you'll get anywhere.'

I ask him if he'll go on climbing, even now?

'My ambition is to keep going and to be walking gently – gently – into my nineties,' he responds ruefully.

I'm so honoured to be walking alongside this great man as we climb the last few metres to the top of the crag. And so, I find, are the couple we meet as we near the top of the path.

'You came and gave a talk at my school in the sixties,' a fair-haired woman says to Sir Chris. 'It was quite inspirational. Can we have a photo with you, please?'

Being the gent he is, this is, of course, no trouble to the 'Boning Meister'. After our impromptu photo call, we plough on, finally reaching a plateau, home to a very unusual sight: dozens, no, hundreds, of pieces of slate, neatly positioned and standing upright, carefully balanced on their edges. They're here because the slopes of the Crag have been extensively quarried. These standing stones are made up of all sorts of sizes and shapes. Someone – or several somebodies – has worked hard to put these in place, here, although exactly why, when or who is all a bit of a mystery. Legend has it, if these were to be knocked over, they would mysteriously re-erect themselves. Perhaps even more mysteriously, Sir Chris has never noticed them before.

'What?!' I exclaim 'How could you miss them?'

'Well, I can only blame something I call "Summit-itis",' he laughs. 'I think I get so focused on getting to the top ["hazard of the job", I think] that I haven't paid enough attention on the way up!'

'You mean I am actually showing Sir Chris Bonington something he hasn't seen on a summit before?' I rib him, as we take the final few steps to the summit proper.

And what a view we're rewarded with. It's hard to believe that we're only about 300m (1,000ft) high. This really is a beautiful spot, with magnificent views across to Derwentwater and Skiddaw to the north and Upper Borrowdale and Great End to the south. You'd normally have to walk three times as far and high for views like this. This Borrowdale walk really does have it all.

As we sit on a mound and take a moment with a glass of bubbly and a bite of Herdwick pasty, the sky looks extraordinary. We can see rain in the distance all around us, but we, ourselves, are bathed in a crown of sunshine. It's glorious. Or as my seventeen-year-old nephew Jack would say, 'sweet-ass amazing beyond all belief'.

No two visits to this magnificent place are ever the same.

Every walk here is a different experience, no matter how many times you do it, because this land of microclimates never offers up the same sky twice in a row. And although I didn't expect to feel any different about Castle Crag this time, because I've always loved it, today I find I love it even more.

What better finish to this walk then a well-deserved picnic with a legendary climber and adventurer, overlooking the 'loveliest square mile in Lakeland'. And then I remember the last time I saw this rather unassuming, yet unique and rugged little peak. It was from up in Mark's helicopter. He knew it was a favourite place and took me on a special flight over it one summer. So, maybe that's where our sunshine has come from today.

'Cheers, Mark,' I murmur and I tip my glass up to the sky.

WALKER'S GUIDE:
WHERE TO STAY, WHERE TO EAT,
WHAT TO SEE, WHAT TO DO

To start: I kicked off with a scone at the Flock In Tea Room, Borrowdale: and very good it was too (Rosthwaite, Keswick CA12 5XB).

To visit: Keswick Pencil Museum: no, really, if you need to be inside in Keswick you couldn't be anywhere more unexpectedly interesting (Main St, Keswick CA12 5NG – http://www.pencilmuseum.co.uk/).

To stay: You're spoiled for choice around Derwentwater. Honister Cottage (Seatoller CA12 5XN – https://curatedby. theoutdoorguide.co.uk/paradigmcottages), the cottages at Skiddaw Hotel, Keswick and the Inn on the Square (Keswick CA12 5JF – https://curatedby.theoutdoorguide.co.uk/ innonthesquare) all come highly recommended.

To see: Herdwick sheep, perhaps at Borrowdale Yew Tree farm. This heritage breed is still a key part of the local landscape thanks to one Beatrix Potter (same place as the tea room above – http://borrowdaleyewtreefarm.co.uk/herdwick/).

6

CUMBRIA: THE HIGH CUP NICK WALK

'Wilderness is a necessity' – John Muir

I've met lots of craftsmen and women on my travels over the years. Annabelle, the smithy we met in Malham, who makes hand-forged candle sconces and bottle openers; others who still build handcrafted wooden boats or handmade brushes. And, I've visited family-owned factories before, where they process crabs or make beauty products out of seaweed, but I've never come across an old school business quite like the one I've found in Dufton, belonging to the Rudds.

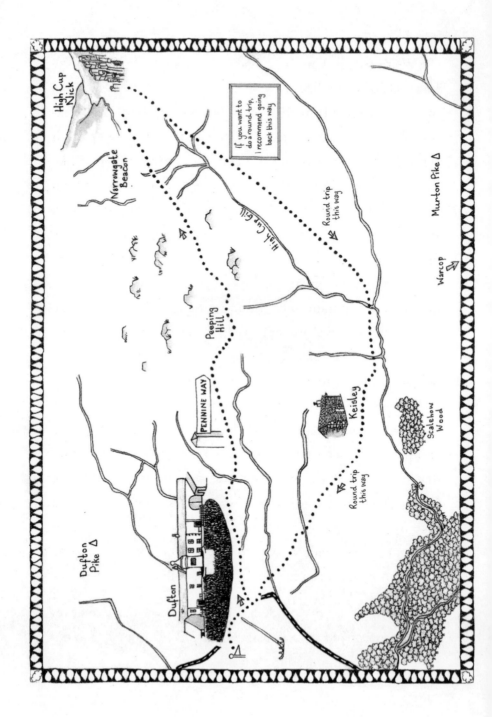

High Cup
Nick

Narrowgate
Beacon

If you want to
do a round-trip,
I recommend going
back this way

Round trip
this way

Murton Pike △

Warcop

High Cup Gill

Peeping
Hill

PENNINE WAY

Keisley

Scalehow
Wood

Round trip
this way

Dufton
Pike △

Dufton

We're still in Cumbria, just 30-odd kilometres from the Lake District. Dufton is a small village of fewer than 200 inhabitants and, like many rural villages of its size, it has a reasonably modern claim to fame. In the eighteenth and nineteenth centuries, this was a mining area, specifically lead mining. Like the internationally renowned company Cadbury, the London Lead Company was Quaker-owned and socially responsible. Part of that obligation included installing, along with solidly built homes and a school for its workers, lead piping to carry water around the village. There's still a rather out-of-place-looking red fountain to be found in the middle of the village green. Although we've changed completely changed our minds about the validity of lead piping and it's not used for water pipes because it's toxic, they did mean well, those Quakers.

The house I'm currently standing outside was built in 1632, before the Quakers. I know this because right above the entrance, there's a stone with the date carved on it declaring that fact. This is the workshop of John Rudd and his son, Graeme, who are traditional rake makers. Yep, that's right: rake makers. Now you may think that there's not much of a market for handmade wooden rakes, but you'd be wrong. The Rudd family has been handcrafting them here since 1890 and they're shipped all over the country. Their rakes have been used as props in big Hollywood movies like *Robin Hood, Prince of Thieves*, starring Morgan Freeman and Kevin Costner.

And they haven't just made film appearances, they also

showed up at London's Olympic Games in 2012. Remember the scene that greeted the visitors to the Olympic Stadium on opening night, with the billions watching around the world? The one that British film director Danny Boyle devotedly created? That impressive image of a bucolic England, fields roaming with sheep and cows and haystacks and men with smocks – and *wooden rakes*? Remember?

'Oh, that's a very complicated affair,' remarks John Rudd, as Colin, the soundman, feeds the microphone wire up his shirt and through an opening in his blue overalls. John's a friendly, affable man in about his sixties, thinning on top, but sprouting a few little extra hairs in other places, if you know what I mean. His is a true family business. He learned the trade from his father, also called John, who himself learned it from his own father before him. Now *this* John's son, Graeme (middle name John), also makes rakes. So, the family have been making rakes for four generations. Graeme's 13-year-old son does help out in the workshop. 'But it's too soon to tell if he's going to follow in our footsteps,' Graeme confides. Rather disappointingly his son is called James.

From the outside, this place looks the very definition of a cottage industry, but they manufacture nearly 500 rakes a month here. In a workshop, behind the ancient little room where we're standing, is a slightly more advanced-looking workbench, but it's not exactly state of the art. The machine on display was put in by John's father, fifty years ago and, as far as mechanising the process goes, that's it. The machine makes the teeth and the holes in the head, no more; everything else is done by hand. They're creating almost exactly the same product in exactly the same way as their grandfather did, and their great grandfather before that. It's really a beautiful throwback in time. I hope young James does pick up the mantle (or rake handle).

Given that the number of hay meadows is shrinking, something we discovered in the Dales, where there are some of the best remaining ones, I ask them where – apart from as props in the occasional movie and at the Olympics – they sell most of their rakes.

'Most of our output goes to Lancashire,' John tells me. 'They get used on major athletic meetings, to rake the sand on long-jump pits, on bunkers on golf courses. Originally they were called hay rakes; that side of the business has gone. Now, they're more multi-purpose; more are sold for putting ready-mix concrete down than for making hay. They're versatile, we've put a long pole on some to pull debris out of duck ponds.'

John's got a dry sense of humour and while the crew are taking some extra shots he asks me whereabouts I live. 'London,' I reply, to which he winces: 'Poor you.'

He brings out an odd-looking rake – at least, it should be a rake, but the head's totally different. 'We had a special order, a one-off from Chester Zoo for a Komodo Dragon stick.'

A Komodo Dragon stick? What's that? There's one bit of wildlife I haven't come across yet and if I ever do, I think I'll be exceptionally cautious. A large snake with legs and a nasty temper. Hmmm.

'What's it for?' I ask.

'To control them.'

Wow. I remember the Komodo Dragons in a James Bond film and I suppose I'd want something to control them if a 68kg (150lb), almost 2m (6ft) carnivorous lizard was coming at me – but I'm pretty sure I'd want more than a wooden pole.

John has some tips for me on my walk. 'Keep an eye out for Nichols' Chair, where it's alleged that a cobbler once sat and repaired a pair of shoes for a wager and listen to this . . .'

He produces a diary written by a mining surveyor called Will Fleming, which belonged to John's grandfather. He reads out the entry dated Tuesday 5 August 1890: 'About 200 people got dinner on High Cup Nick.' That's the place where I'm going. I like the idea of a picnic for 200 people up the top of a hill. That would have taken an awful lot of organizing. But why did they do it? Were they celebrating something? Or was it just for fun? There's no doubt life in the country would have been tough back then, so something like that picnic, so out of the ordinary, would have been a real treat. For whoever wasn't making all those sandwiches, anyway. Glad it wasn't me.

I leave the Rudds with a warm fuzzy feeling inside and I've bought myself two rakes: one for my garden at home in London and one as a birthday present for my mate, Matt Baker. He'll bloody love it. A hand-made wooden rake especially for his little smallholding in Hertfordshire. Now that's what I call bespoke!

I'm really enjoying being back outdoors filming the walks. I'm now about six weeks in and I'm feeling good, just a bit tired from all the travelling. As folk often remark, 'You get paid to do what millions of people do every week for pleasure,' which is walk. Yep. And I'm passionate about it, getting people away from their tellies (yes, ironic, I know) and getting some fresh air in their lungs.

Barely a week goes by without some new research revealing that walking can quite literally save your life:

'Walking a mile a day can cut risk of dying from cancer by 40%.'

'Twenty-minute walk each day adds seven years to your life.'

'Research shows that walking 10,000 steps a day will significantly improve your health. Walking can build stamina and give you a healthier heart.'

'A stroll by the sea will help you sleep longer, study finds.' All real headlines.

Walking can also help relieve stress, improve concentration, help heal depression and it can inspire you to be more creative. And the great thing is, obviously, you can do it anywhere. Once you've mastered the gentle art of putting one foot in front of the other – and it won't be too long before I'm having to help my two little girls do just that, now that their older brother is fully practised at it – then you can walk wherever you like. Along the side of canals, through a local park, over a bridge, up a hill, along the edge of fields (closing the gate behind you as you go, of course!) or, if you are ready to take it up a level, set out on a proper hike, through rough country along tracks that are only just visible. Sweet.

I hope I'm going to be doing it well into my eighties like Sir Chris Bonington, my Castle Crag companion. (I posted a photo on Twitter a couple of months after our climb and he posted back, 'A happy reminder of doing you on top of one of Lakeland's best viewpoints. The champagne was a plus.' (I don't think he meant it quite like that, but I understood the sentimentand it caused quite a few chuckles! Sir Chris has subsequently blamed the horror of the 21st century that is autocorrect. "I'd meant 'join' Julia on Castle Crag. I blush." We've all been there, haven't we?) That's why I'm involved with walking and outdoor groups, businesses and charities like the Camping and Caravanning Club, Ramblers Worldwide Holidays and the Wainwright Society. You don't have to be a crazy fool enthusiast to appreciate the outdoors and enjoy it a bit.

So the walks are a real pleasure for me but the experience of *filming* them – and not just walking the route for 'lee-joor', as our American friends say – is different. Some of the time at least. Once again, due to traffic, weather and time constraints, we have to film the programme out of sequence, which means as soon as we arrive we have to hop out of one car and into another in order to film one portion up on top of the hills. We all pile into some old Land Rover Defenders (Landys), the only vehicle up to the job on this sort of terrain, and make our way up to the top. It's freezing cold, the sky is grey and the rain is not quite at full pelt. Everything goes well and by the time we finish, all in all we've got about four hours' worth of filming done. Not bad after a five-hour road trip. Day One. In the bag.

It's a weird thing, filming where the general public can see you. I often joke that 'this' – the green all around me – is my office. Not many people get watched over in their office by complete strangers. People are curious, of course, and some people have lots of questions, while others just nod and move along.

This evening our long day leads to a somewhat irritating conversation outside the pub. A group of walkers are standing about, watching us rushing around, unloading the vehicles. Then they all start asking questions about the programme, when it will be screened, that sort of thing; someone asks what the series is going to be called. Before I have a chance to reply, this guy butts in – 'should be called Julia Bradbury's Land Rover Walks, *fnar fnar*'. Very funny.

Anyway, I hope by now you're getting itchy feet of your own as you read this book, and are already planning when you can pull on your boots and start meandering through a country lane or striding up and down a hill or two. If you haven't yet, then I'm prepared to bet that you will after this walk, also in Cumbria, because it's a real beauty. It's also probably one of the least well-known walks that I'm featuring here.

We're deep in the heart of wild Britain, at a place that is

very close to one of the most visited locations in Europe – the Lake District. We've already walked around Borrowdale and Derwentwater and yet, even though it's not that far distance-wise – in fact it's the shortest distance between walks featured in this book – only a fraction of the tourists who visit the Lakes, come to High Cup Nick every year. And I find that odd because it's every bit as spectacular, beautiful, uplifting and exciting as anything the Lakes have to offer. It also has the unusual honour of being the only place in the country that has a wind named specially for the region – the infamous Helm Wind.

High Cup Nick is unusually named, in the same way that Barf (a fell in the Lake District) or Lord Hereford's Knob (a mountain in south-east Wales) are. You come across such places in the countryside. I always think that an unusual name helps you remember the experience more and I won't forget this one, certainly, in the Pennines. Although we're still in the same county, Cumbria, it's a wholly different place to where we visited in Chapter 5. The open land on top of the Pennines feels wilder. They may have filmed *Star Wars* at Derwentwater, but I bet you anything that the location scouts didn't see this place. It's often called the Grand Canyon of the Pennines and you'll see why later.

Before I head for the hills, I just want to make sure I don't get shot. We're close to a Ministry of Defence training area, you see, in the nearby village of Warcop. It's been an Army training base since the Second World War and in use constantly since then. So if you hear the pitter patter of gunfire in the air you know what's going on. At the edge of Dufton, at what's known as 'Town Head', you'll see a small metal flagpole right next to an ugly big yellow road salt dispenser. If the red flag is flying, it means they're training, so watch yourself. It may seem unexpected but there are MOD-training areas in some of our most rugged and wild areas. I made it all the way to Cape Wrath near Durness in north-west Scotland once, which is referred to as 'the last great wilderness' because of its remoteness. It's a stunning stretch of severe but beautiful upland moorland and it also happens to be the only range in Europe where land, sea and air training activities can be done simultaneously. It's so remote the Royal Air Force can train using live 453kg (1,000lb) bombs! You'd better be on the watch for that red flag if you go hiking there!

Also at Town Head, just up the lane, are two old gents, Frank and Harry, who have lived here since before the Army came. Harry I'll talk about later. Frank's in his fifties and has been here since he was five, so he should be the perfect candidate to tell me little bit more about what to expect once I've left the confines of the village. On our first day, Frank helped us get to the top of the Nick in his Landy. Handily, he's the only person who knows the area and, in particular, the higher ground, well enough *not* to drive off a terrifying cliff or get stuck in a bog. He has a face that can only be described as ruddy and has rather wild looking eyes and a shock of upright, unruly white hair, all of which can make for quite an alarming first impression. I think he'd definitely be a suspect in an episode of *Midsomer Murders* but turn out not to be the killer.

What I'm trying to say is Frank is a distinctly quirky individual. And he's a man of few words as I was about to learn. Every day that he films with us, he turns up wearing the same bottle green short-sleeved polo shirt – or maybe it's variations on a theme. And it's freezing. The rest of us are wearing thermals and hats up on the moors, but not Frank. He's obviously not much mithered by the Helm Wind, as they say in these parts.

I want to know more about the Helm Wind, which apparently can last for days and is completely unique to this area. With swirling gusts of up to 80 miles per hour, the Helm Wind has swept animals and people off their feet for centuries. Legend has it that the wind assisted the English defences by knocking the Norman cavalry off their horses during the reign of William the Conqueror. The geological combination of the Pennines, lower pikes and easterly winds all help generate the turbulence and the locals know it's coming when a rolling bar of cloud appears above the fells, which looks a bit like a helmet forming on the mountain tops. Apparently it makes a roaring noise like a speeding train.

When I ask Frank about it, he underplays it entirely: 'Nowt serious,' Frank says, before adding, 'Times we've had to climb gates because you couldn't open them, it was blowing that hard.' Really? Is that it?!

On our way down the fell after filming on the first day, we came across the most endearing black fell ponies, which we stopped to film. Frank's family own those ponies, so to link the two pieces together I want Frank to tell me a bit about them in this chat.

'So Frank, how likely is it that I'm going to see some fell ponies up there?' I ask him.

'I don't know,' he replies.

'Cut! No Frank, I *know* that I AM going to see them because we've already filmed them,' I explain. 'So can you tell me something like there's a good chance?' Jan, the cameraman, starts filming again.

'So Frank, how likely is it that I'm going to see some fell ponies up there?'

'Not that likely. Depends where you go exactly.'

'Cut. Can you just tell me there's a possibility?' I plead. 'Here we go . . . so, Frank, how likely is it that I'm going to see some fell ponies up there?' I ask again.

'You might be lucky. There's 1,200 acres for them to run round in!' He rubs his hands together, very pleased with himself.

'Thank you, Frank. Wonderful.'

And so are these ponies. Watching these endearing animals, I feel like I'm taking part in an ad for a bank. A string of little black beauties gallop across the horizon through the tall grass. For nearly 300 years these ponies were working horses, working the farmland and carrying lead ore from the mines. These days they simple 'are', roaming free and looking pretty. A rarity in country life, they actually have no purpose - they're not even broken so you can't ride them. They're simply here because of tradition.

I carry on walking up the country lane, past the farm at Bow Hall in the direction of the Pennine Way trail. As I mentioned the Helm Wind is the *only* named wind in Britain, so I'm going to use that as a cue to talk about walking and the weather. Of all the walks I'm going on for this series, it's on this one that you're most exposed to the elements. You're in 't 'North oop 'ere' – and there isn't a lot of shelter at the top of the Pennines so be prepared. I would describe this moorland landscape as one of the wildest in England, it's truly unspoilt and remote. Here, I think you get the true sense of naturalness. It's not an Area of Outstanding Natural Beauty for nothing. The resident population of the area in a 1997 Natural England report was recorded as 12,000 people. I don't think it's gone up much in twenty odd years, making it one of the least populated parts of England. It also has one of the harshest climates. Nearby Cross Fell is *the* coldest place known in the north of England. You've been warned. I am wearing pants over pants with thermals, but the Greek in me tends to feel the cold more than most, so you may be all right with just one layer of 'pantage'.

I like walking in all weathers. It's always gorgeous to walk along the coast in the sunshine (not least because you know you're going to sleep well that night), the sun warming you on your way, but it's also gratifying to crunch down a country lane in the frost, your breath steaming out in front of you. The truth is, it's great to be outdoors in almost any weather – so long as you're prepared and dressed for it. About the only kind of weather I really don't like walking in is when it's wet from beginning to end. Then it's time to split and go and closely analyse the local infusions at the nearest saloon.

I'm now up in the countryside proper, a couple of kilometres into the walk. I'm heading up a steady hill, surrounded by green fields, sectioned off by what seems endless drystone walling. Looking back, the hills roll down as far as the eye can see. From here Murton Pike and Dufton Pike, two beautifully formed hills, frame the Eden Valley in the distance. I carry on climbing a small grassy dome, which has the lovely name of Peeping Hill. High Cup Nick itself is still well hidden from view, but Peeping Hill is the first place you get to. Well, peep at it.

On my way up I bump into an offcumden called Julie Sandilands, who's a novelist from Cheshire. She seems to lead a pretty idyllic life. She's a secondary school English teacher from Kinross High School in Perth and she comes here to write during the school holidays, taking her inspiration from the landscape and its 'timeless quality'. Her tales of trolls, Viking warriors and missing swords are fuelled by Cumbrian folk tales and traditions and she's distilled them into three children's books: *Finn's Tales*, *A Tale of Tinkers Trolls and Troublemakers* and *A Gypsy's Tale*.

'The dream is to live here permanently,' she tells me. 'There's a real community here. It felt like home very quickly. There are beer festivals, art festivals . . . I feel like an honorary Cumbrian.'

Sitting next to Julie is what looks like a fell pony. Sort of. It's actually a giant dog called Ollie, the kind I've never seen before – a Deerhound crossed with a Standard Poodle. He's quite lovely and not surprisingly he's the star of her next series of books, the not surprisingly named 'Ollie Dog' books.

'You must feel pretty safe walking across the moors with him,' I laugh.

'Yes, I don't get bothered much!' she admits.

I turn to leave Julie and Ollie to plot their next book together, but before I go I turn back to Julie and ask if she's come across the infamous Helm Wind. I'm hoping for a better account than Frank's.

'Noooo!' she exclaims. 'I thought I had one day, when I was making my way up here, but the landlady said, "Nay lass, 's'not t'Helm Wind. T'Helm Wind blows turnips out of fields."' Blimey. Sounds painful.

I carry on towards the top of Peeping Hill. There's evidence here of the land being worked – a communal drystone wall sheep pen and an old lime kiln. Most of the land up here is in hill farming use these days, grazed by sheep or cattle or it's managed as grouse moor. The North Pennines are, in fact, world famous for their outstanding mineral veins and deposits and mining these minerals has had a profound effect on the landscape. Everywhere you look you can see the legacy of mining – from spoil heaps, mine shafts and chimneys to the area's pattern of settlements. Lead mining may have been the principal industry, but there's evidence of coal workings, iron-stone mining, quarrying and peat cutting dotted everywhere, too. The lime kiln here would have been used to heat limestone and produce quicklime. All the early civilizations used it in building mortars and as a stabilizer in mud renders and floors. It must have been an unpleasant job though, working on the kiln in those days. No 'elf and safety and a big risk of chemical burns from the quicklime.

As we continue up the hill (and I've got to admit my thighs are now burning), Jan spots a glider in the air. 'Bloody hell, I've got the wrong lens on.' He scrabbles to get the camera off his back and onto the tripod which Alex the director is carrying, so he can try and get a shot of the plane. I do a pathetic little wave up to the sky, but it's a tiny blob by now.

The Helm Wind has some good uses, it seems. Glider pilots love it round here; they use the wind to gain height at a rate of 300m to 600m (1,000ft to 2,000ft) per minute! And they can get up to an altitude of more than 6,000m (20,000ft). I've been in a glider a couple of times, once over Berlin and once over the pastoral Oxfordshire countryside. It's a fairly awesome experience seeing the earth from that high up with just a 'whooshing' sound for company. The topography of the Pennines must look pretty special from up there.

The landscape has become more boulder-strewn now. I can see rocky limestone outcrops all around me. Plenty of trip hazards. And I can also see a little girl holding hands with her mum on the brow of the hill in front of me. That must be Dr Charlotte Adams and her daughter, Sophie.

When you read about High Cup Nick you come across phrases like 'spectacular geographical feature' or 'impressive glaciated U-shaped valley' and you may want to ask, why? Well, Dr Adams is a geologist and lecturer at Durham University and she can explain that better than most. And like most people who are really good at their job, she's very passionate about what she does.

'I first came here when I was sixteen, on a GCSE geology field trip,' she recalls. 'One look at this place and I was smitten. By the end of the day I had a bag full of rocks that I took home. I probably didn't realize how hooked I'd become – I've been working in geology ever since. There's so much going on in a relatively small space and it all started here.'

I ask her to tell me about the geology of the area in layman's terms.

'It's amazing the things that have been deposited here over geological time. Some of the oldest rocks in the Pennines, around 500 million years old, are just behind us; while some

of the youngest ones are down in the Eden valley, big boulders
of material brought here by the glaciers and dumped by the
ice sheets as they travelled over the land, left behind when the
ice melted. The landscape was really shaped by a combination
of all the agents: water, wind, fire, ice.'

The oldest rocks were formed when two continental plates
smashed against one other, creating the base rock, granite,
which is known here as 'Weardale Granite'. In the millennia
that followed, the North Pennines area was periodically covered
with shallow seas and forests. As sea levels rose and fell, rock
layers of limestone, shale, sandstone and coal were formed and
were added to on top by red sandstone, when the land dried
out. At some point, as the great layers of granite cooled and
cracked, shafts appeared and another of the distinctive features
of the area was formed, as Charlotte continues to explain:

'We've got a bit of the Whin Sill behind us as well, a
molten sheet of granite pushed into the middle of all these
existing sedimentary rocks, almost like prying apart the leaves
of a book. The rock intruded into the landscape and, further
beyond that, into the valley.'

The last Ice Age was a good deal more recent. Only 20,000
years ago (only!) ice nearly a kilometre thick would have covered the surface of the Pennines. This, Charlotte tells me, is
what brought about the change in the landscape and shaped
what we know as the majestic High Cup Nick:

'The reason we can see it today is, when the glaciers moved

over the land, they took a massive gouge out of the ground, so they effectively chiselled a massive area, that we can see now.'

Ice is incredible, isn't it? Next time you order that Grey Goose on the rocks or a Magners think about High Cup Nick, millions of years in the forming, ultimately created by frozen water.

'Had an ice sheet not moved through this area,' Charlotte reiterates, 'and taken a great slice out of it, you probably never would have been able to see what we see today.'

Charlotte is a sweetie; solidly knowledgeable, impassioned, warm and approachable. I imagine her lectures are thoroughly engrossing. I ask her if she's working on a particular project at the moment.

'We're looking at using deep geothermal energy, from a variety of sources, and one of those is abandoned mines. This area was really important because they mined lead here; we're going back into these mines again because they contain water – many of them were flooded after they were closed. We can take the heat out of that water, and use that to heat homes and businesses throughout the UK.'

Wow. Nothing much then. Only a solution to the world energy crisis. I look at Charlotte's daughter, Sophie, wrapped up snuggly against the elements; a scarf wound around her little neck like a coiled pipe cleaner, hat pulled down almost covering her eyes. She must be so proud of her mum the 'rock' star. Will she follow in her footsteps?

'We're training her,' Charlotte laughs. I'd say this was a valuable day off school.

I thank them both, we do the selfie thing and Colin, the soundman, removes the microphone packs and wires, which is never easy when they're submerged under multiple layers of fleece and feather down jackets. Colin has been doing this since he qualified with a 2:1 in Media Production at Northumbria University, but he still gets embarrassed 'fertling' as we call it.

Now that I'm fully informed about what's been going on beneath our boots, I want to see one of those elemental forces I've just been hearing about at work. Luckily the Ice Age has passed, the volcanoes are long dead and the wind's not blowing, but the water's still flowing. With spectacular vistas behind me, out to Dufton and Murton Pike, I continue through the boulder fields and follow the path to the head of the valley, edging closer to the valley below. I can just see the rim of High Cup Nick on my right, but not down into the deep cut, so it's difficult to work out any scale just yet. The narrowest part is appropriately named Narrow Gate and is squashed between the valley rim and Hannah's Well. This spring forms the source of Strands Beck, one of the many feeders of High Cup Gill – the ribbon-like river running right through the middle of the valley below. Strands Beck descends southwards into the gorge and I expect to find a gentle stream, given the sweet name of Hannah's Well – and because the last time the crew came to visit on the recce earlier in the year, that's what was here. Today, thanks to the recent rains, it's an obstacle to negotiate. A gushing, overflowing, loud watery obstacle. The water's actually spurting down the hill and raucously tumbling into the valley below. I have a thing about rushing water. If I'm wearing waterproof boots – which I am – I can't resist having a splash about. There's just something so satisfying about your feet being engulfed in the water and not getting wet. I wade back and forth like a child. At least the boots work.

You can imagine that I have a LOT of gear. Over the years I have amassed quite a collection, but outdoor kit can be addictive because there's always a new technology to test: this keeps you drier; this keeps you hotter; this cools you down; this wicks; this regulates your body; this regulates your mind (now that would be good) – seriously though, it's never ending. So for these walks, I've been trying out some new *Arc'teryx* boots (alongside my favourite Mammut GTX specials), which have a stretch Gore-Tex liner and a 'thermolaminated single seamless upper'. The words 'permeable for ventilation' and 'hydrophobic' pop up in the description too. They're meant to be waterproof and they are. They're meant to be super comfortable and they are. My advice to people considering new boots is *never* to embark on a long walk in a brand new pair – always break them in and take your time and the right socks with you when you do choose to try them out. These are your best friends on a hike. I love my Jimmy Choo's but mostly they just look pretty.

These narrow rocky paths and engorged streams are testing

enough in daylight when you're walking carefully and paying close attention to the terrain. Think how much worse it would be in the dark. Running. Because that's what the person I'm meeting now has spent some considerable time doing. I can honestly say I've never been tempted to run the length of the Pennine Way, non-stop, but back in 1989 that's exactly what Mike Hartley did. He ran the 412km (256 miles) miles of Britain's longest national trail in just two days, seventeen hours and twenty minutes – averaging almost 144km (90 miles) per day. No sleep for the swift. I ask him how on earth he managed it. And, more importantly, why?

Mike's a gentle, soft-spoken man, who clearly has a love of the outdoors, even if he goes past it faster than Jeremy Clarkson road-testing a Ferrari California T. 'It's hard to believe I did it, looking back twenty-six years. Just practice, lots of practice,' he says, adding, 'You need a good torch.'

No shit, Sherlock. I think I'd wear car headlights strapped to my chest.

It's worth stressing again what an extraordinary achievement Mike's run is. Billy the fell-runner's achievements are extraordinary but this is the Pennine Way. Experienced walkers would be aiming to complete a passage of it in two, possibly three weeks – mostly, of course, because they'd be sensibly tucked up in bed at night. Mike, in contrast, would be out running in the dark along trails that I'm treading carefully on today. How on earth does he cope with it at speed?

'The most difficult bits you may have to jog and walk,' he replies. 'Where you can, you run, but you've got to look after yourself on the more awkward bits. In the right frame of mind, you can do okay. That two days, seventeen hours and twenty minutes is non-stop. There's no sleep, just a few minutes' rest at road crossings. When the average walker's in his B&B overnight, I'm knocking out another seventy miles.' But he's not all gung-ho. 'Take it easy, being careful. It's a progressive thing, obviously you go out and do shorter runs at night, maybe half a night, until you're ready for the Pennine Way. That's two complete nights of running non-stop.'

I think I'm looking slightly slack jawed at this stage. 'Okay, I've got the *how*, but . . . *why?*'

Mike's answer is that it's about the challenge. As to why he rose to it: 'It's the longest, most famous run in the UK. I'd done a lot of other ones, shorter ones, up to 200 miles.' *Shorter . . . 200-mile runs . . . right, I thought to myself.* 'This, being the most famous, had to be the cherry on the cake, really. It's about testing myself, keep pushing further, harder. I have a certain amount of stubbornness, really. If I get tired, or injured, and don't want to do it, the disappointment that would come from failing would be worse – so it seems worth putting up with the pain, the agony . . . rather than the disappointment of failure. It's a particular mindset. I don't like failing things; I don't like getting things wrong. I like to prepare to the last degree and success is more likely, then.'

'It's worked so far, then. You're still the record holder,' I say, pointing out the obvious.

Mike smiles ruefully. 'Nobody else has been daft enough so far!' But he thinks it won't be too long before someone does have a go and, when they do, he'll be there.

'To cheer them on – or to trip them up?' I suggest mischievously to Mike's amusement. Then he tells me he enjoys coming back to a place like this, a special marker on the run, when he can take the time to look about him and enjoy the view. I ask him if he's made the trip up to High Cup Nick often.

'Oh, yeah, many times.'

I know that Mike was bitten by the long-distance bug and ran the Coast to Coast, as well – he also holds the record for that. 'I think you're just a little bit insane,' I tell him, 'but I'm full of admiration for you.'

Mike's running days are behind him – I think – but he's got one last thing to say about High Cup Nick as we part ways: 'It's one of the highlights of the Pennine Way. You're going to love it.'

That's what I keep hearing and the anticipation is killing me. 'Thanks, Mike,' I say as I leave him to begin my final leg.

To add to the drama of the landscape we have a bit of drama of our own. The sun is dropping faster than a plunging lapwing. If we don't make it to the Nick before sunset then we'll have to do the entire walk again tomorrow, just to get the final five minutes of the programme. I've already explained how much I love walking and if we were doing it all again for pleasure I'd be thrilled, but we have other things to film (they're called 'pick-ups') and coming back all this way again will cost us hours and hours. Alex marches on ahead. I'm walking in her footsteps, thinking through what I'm going to say when I finally get to our goal and I see High Cup for the first time. Jan pulls the camera bag onto his back and strides out the kilometre or so we've still got to go. Colin positions his 'electric handbag', as I call it, in the most comfortable position around his waist for walking (there isn't one really – there never is with any handbag), and Frank, still dressed in his short-sleeved bottle green polo shirt, oblivious to the biting wind, tells us he'll wait for us.

I am not disappointed. The full splendour of High Cup Nick is quite heavenly. A craggy, rocky edge frames either side of a huge deep U-shaped gulch and because the sun is falling the whole spectacle is changing colour in front of my eyes. An expanse of greens, golds and burnt reds stand out against the horizon. The masculine features of this natural wonder look even more arresting as the valley becomes shrouded in shadow. The Grand Canyon of the Pennines. You're not kidding. It's vast – this stunning deep hollow. The sunlight flashes off the silvery gill running below. The ground just drops away offering up immense intense views of the glistening Eden Valley in the distance. It's mesmerizing. When I got my job in Hollywood I went via an assignment at the Grand Canyon in Arizona. You never forget an encounter with something so utterly incredible; it's a memory that gets lodged in the back of the mind only to return again and again throughout your life. It seems a long time ago now and I think to myself how funny life is, the twists and turns that lead you to your destiny. 'From Hollywood to High Cup Nick,' I laugh under my breath.

To the side is an isolated pinnacle of granite, like some sort of chimney leading up from the bowels of the Earth below. This is Nichol's Chair and if a cobbler did shin up there to settle a wager, good on him – personally, I don't fancy it. I do envy the 200 people who came up here to picnic on that August day in 1890 though, thinking back to the entry that John Rudd read me from Will Fleming's diary. What an absolutely gorgeous spot for a gathering like that.

In the distance, not so far away, the Lake District winks knowingly in our direction. Funny to think that millions of people go there, while this magnificent place is barely known. What an oversight – this is one of the highlights of the Pennine Way, one described by Wainwright as an 'unforgettable sight'. This Great Big View make you feel very small, indeed, and very happy to be alive. And even though this is a good testing walk, this colossal chasm, off a wild Pennine moor, is beyond an incentive to do it. Towering columns and vertical cliffs formed 295 million years ago generally require much more exertion. Ask Sir Chris Bonington.

At the beginning of this chapter, I mentioned an old boy

called Harry who's been friends with Frank since they were both wee. They've lived around here most of their lives and Harry has reached the impressive age of ninety-three. As I stand in this mesmerizing place, I think of him and how much has changed during his lifetime, his ninety-three years. This is a place that brings on those kind of thoughts. When he was a young lad, his parents couldn't afford to keep Harry, to clothe and feed him, so he was sold off to a local farmer as a farmhand in about 1936. As shocking as that sounds, it was a quite common occurrence back then. In fact, it happened to my grandmother, who was betrothed and 'sold' to the Greek grandfather I never met in Cardiff, also in the 1930s. Society was different, the country was in the grips of economic depression and barely anyone, except the wealthy, had electricity. The nation was made up of subsistence farmers; meat was scarce and dinner, for the vast majority, would have largely consisted of bread, butter and potatoes.

Despite his early circumstances though, Harry couldn't be happier. 'Oh, I've had a good life,' he tells me. And you can tell he really means it.

Standing here looking out on to this dizzying view I think about Harry and about all the changes he's seen and those that will happen in my own children's lifetimes. If you'd have told Harry in the 1930s that we'd all be carrying mini computers around with us, video chatting and flying thousands of kilo-metres around the globe in just a few hours, I'm sure it would have seemed incomprehensible. So much has changed, but the one thing that hasn't in all that time is High Cup Nick. It's still here for us all to enjoy, still standing strong and magnificent after millions of years. And now, as I stand here pondering nature, I wonder if my own babes will come and stand in exactly this same spot, gazing, as I am, out on to this otherworldly precipice.

Well if they do, I think, I really hope they Skype me.

WALKER'S GUIDE:
WHERE TO STAY, WHERE TO EAT,
WHAT TO SEE, WHAT TO DO

To finish: You couldn't do better than a pint at the Stag Inn (Dufton, Appleby, Cumbria CA16 6DB – https://curatedby. theoutdoorguide.co.uk/thestagdufton) – and the attached cottage is a wonderful place to stay, just a stumble from the pub.

To shop: Rudd's Rakes, an amazing survival of local craftsmanship, as seen in the 2012 Olympic Opening Ceremony! (https://www.facebook.com/ruddsrakes/)

To stay: Another good overnight choice in the area is the Tufton Arms Hotel (Market Square, Appleby in Westmorland CA16 6XA – https://curatedby.theoutdoorguide.co.uk/tuftonarms).

To do: If you're feeling tougher than me, you could try running the 412km of the Pennine Way. The record is under three days, running non-stop. Good luck!

7

THE SOUTH DOWNS:
THE BIRLING GAP WALK

'Mind The (Birling) Gap'

When we arrive at the hotel in Eastbourne – a giant wedding cake of a building – where we're staying before
we head off on the South Downs walk, we have, as usual, a little
meet and greet with Jackie Webley, the marketing manager.

Jackie hands me a handsome coffee table book about the
hotel, full of lovely old photos and history and what a history.
Winston Churchill stayed here; the composer Debussy finished
his symphony *La Mer* in Suite 200, in 1905; and Charlie Chaplin

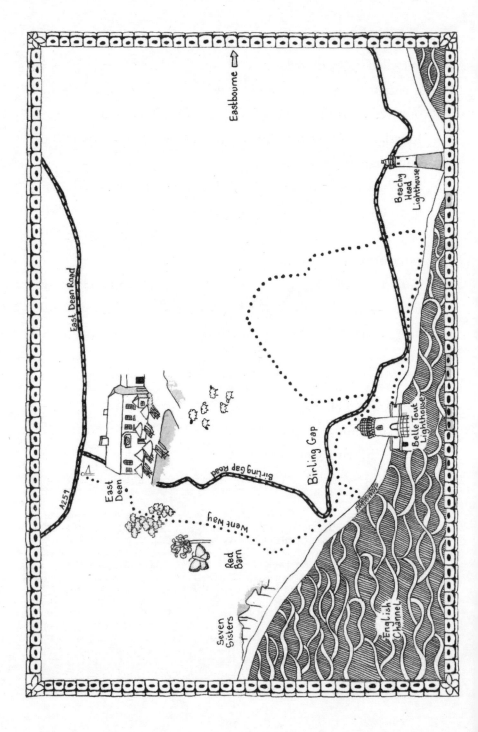

waddled down these lavish corridors in years gone by. (Ooohh, if *only* these walls could talk.) Jackie and I start to chat about our lives – babies, children and careers. She and her husband Jonathan have lived on site at the hotel for twenty-two years, with their son, Charlie.

She affectionately recalls the time when four-year-old Charlie's class was asked to draw his house at school. Her little boy naturally created a masterpiece that lovingly detailed the exterior of the White Palace (as the hotel is also known): there must be at least 300 windows on the front of this hotel. All his little friends thought he was making it up. I imagine it must have been similar to when the Princes William and Harry were asked to draw their house.

When I whizz out of the hotel's brass revolving doors, I wish I was on holiday. The sun is blazing and if we didn't have a walk to film, I'd be in that outdoor pool faster than you can shout 'show us your tan lines!' Never mind, it's still the best job in the world, I tell myself, as I greedily snort up as much sea air as I can.

It may strike you as odd that we're in Eastbourne, when the walk is actually on the South Downs, but the town is the closest we can get to our start point and East Dean is only a few kilometres away. Besides, I like staying by the seaside. Not far from here, nestled among some of the most iconic hills in the country, is the Devil's Dyke, a v-shaped valley, about 90m (300ft) deep, which is the longest, deepest and widest 'dry' valley in Britain. The locals will tell you, confidently, that it was made by the scouring action of glaciers, but they're wrong. Geologists state that it was made when the ground was frozen, as was the chalk underneath, and, when the ground thawed, it slid away under its own weight. Rivers, formed by the melting snow, added to the friction effect of the waterlogged material, creating the valley.

I prefer the old story for the reason behind why it's called the Devil's Dyke. The Devil took offence at the sight of the many churches springing up on the Weald (an Old English word for 'wood'). The forest covered a large swathe of land (essentially modern-day Sussex, Hampshire, Kent and Surrey) and the Devil schemed to dig a trench to the water's edge so that the sea would rush in, drowning everything in its path as it did so. The Devil – clearly not that bright, but not afraid of a bit of manual labour – set to and started digging. What he hadn't counted on was the spirit of local resistance. To repel the Devil, the ultimate defence was deployed: an old woman with a sieve, a candle and a cockerel. Of course. Actually in some versions of the story she's a saint, but I rather like the idea of an old woman setting things to rights. Learning of the Devil's plan, she propped up her candle behind the sieve – so that the light looked like the rays of the rising sun – and prodded and poked her cockerel to make it crow. The Devil, fooled into thinking the night was over and dawn was breaking (told you he was a tool, er, fool), fled before he had the time to finish his work. Not one for seeing things through to the bitter end, was he? Anyway that's how Devil's Dyke was formed. Really.

I mention Devil's Dyke not just because it's such an important part of the topography of the area, but also because a recent study by the Sussex Centre for Folklore has revealed that areas within this national park could be home to 80 per cent more fairies and one-third more ghosts than the average across east and west England. Mythology *and* geology are so important around here.

One thing that's undeniable is this place is beautiful. The painter John Constable called it 'the grandest view in the world'. Visitors are granted amazing views over the Downs out to the sea, and, if you're lucky enough to come here on a clear day, a view as far out as the Isle of Wight. If you're one of the paragliders soaring overhead, then you can probably see even further, way out across the Channel – but I'm not going to give that another go, thank you. The last paragliding pilot I flew with in Corsica smashed into a cliff and shattered almost every bone in his body. He's lucky to be alive. (I've definitely become more risk averse since becoming a mum.)

When you think of the South Downs, you probably picture sloping hills, covered with a lovely green carpet of wild grasses, closely cropped by animals, but when I first hiked across the Downs, many years ago, I noticed something immediately different underfoot, my boots picking up lots of white dust from the chalk surface that makes up so much of the countryside here. You have to imagine the land here buried deep under the ocean, millions of years ago, as countless numbers of small, shelled creatures lived and died in the seas, their shells falling to the bottom, where – after aeons had passed – they were pulverized and crushed into the chalk rock we know today. The land was heavily forested by us humans, who cleared it for the grazing animals. That's why the Downs are so open and why the surface is covered not just with grass, but also with a complex weave of plant life, including all sorts of wonderfully named lovelies like bastard toadflax, salad burnet and squinancywort. 'Squinancy' is an old English word for sore throat (quinsy = tonsillitis) and 'wort' means flower or plant, so the translation is 'sore throat plant'. It used to be taken as a medicinal herb although I'm not sure about the current guidelines on gargling with it these days.

There isn't any squinancywort underfoot, however, on this pristine village green where I'm currently standing. Just perfectly manicured, closely clipped grass. Like many of the villages I've visited, East Dean, where I'm starting the walk, genuinely looks like a film set. I sit down on a pub bench at The Tiger Inn, in the midst of an impeccable collection of flint and brick thatched cottages, to read my script for today's walk. Where the bright sunlight flares off the walls, the flint of the cottage walls seem to give off a blueish tint that's reflected in the colour of the sky. It's an archetypal Sussex scene and this late September hot spell is casting its sunshiny radiance over everything. Thoughts and ideas buzzing through my head, I stand up and make my way out of this idyll to set off on the Went Way, said to be one of England's oldest walking routes. Within a couple of minutes, I catch my first look at the Downs through a gateway and, very unusually, I can clearly make out the end point of today's walk – the Belle Tout Lighthouse.

To my left, I spy a row of fertile looking allotments. Spade in action, tending to some rhubarb, is Mark Proctor, who looks a little bit like Alan Carr in gardening clothes. Mark is a local gardener who seems to work for most of the folk around here and writes an amusing blog under the cunning pseudonym Mark The Gardener. I'm sure no one knows it's him with a name like that, so he can get away with saying all sorts about the people he works for and his gardening exploits: 'Mrs T looked a bit rough when she opened the door this morning . . . but her crocuses are blooming,' that sort of thing. (I wrote that, Mrs T, not Mark, so please don't give him a hard time.)

Mark has been working incredibly hard on a beautiful 300-year-old walled garden that you can see from the village green. The garden's design is true to the original Georgian layout, divided into quarters by gravelled paths with a fountain in the centre. It serves as both a kitchen garden for the property owners, while also providing veg to some of the local spots like The Tiger Inn (almost next door) and hops to the Beachy Head

Brewery. That's the very definition of locally sourced food on your plate. I like.

The Beachy Head area has a murky history as a haven for smugglers. Because of the high taxes on imports, such as tea and alcohol, already luxury items, smuggling was once commonplace, so while you may think of it today as the work of dodgy criminals, historically very often entire villages were in cahoots, helping the smugglers escape the customs men. James Dippery, the former owner of the house with the walled garden, made a fortune from smuggling. When he was arrested, he turned King's Evidence on his associates in return for his freedom. Snitch.

'So, the house and garden were built on *dirty* money – literally?' I tease Mark.

Mark smiles. 'It's a lovely place to work,' he says. 'There is a lot of history . . . I'm still digging the dirt but these days, it's just the soil in the garden that's dirty!'

All this juicy history in such a tiny little parish . . . Mark's an easy-going bloke who tells a good story and he looks utterly at home in this allotment. I can't imagine him doing anything else and yet in his previous incarnation as Mark One he had a different life: 'I used to work at a debt collection company on the personnel side. One of the directors said I could be like him in a couple of years and I had an epiphany: I realized it was time to get out!' One of his favourite local jobs is helping a group of local ladies manage their allotments. They're known, he tells me with a smile, as 'the Babes with Spades'.

On his blog, Mark writes about much more than gardening: it's about reflecting on your life and making it the best it can be. After a beautiful poem by William Martin about making the ordinary things in life come alive, Mark notes: 'The period between the 21st and 27th of June is always a time of quiet reflection, interspersed with wild celebration and this year is no different. The 21st is the 32nd anniversary of my father's death and the 26th is my mother's birthday. [T]he poem above sort of sums up the upbringing they gave me. My mum always said, "It doesn't matter to me if you become a dustman, as long as you are the best dustman you can possibly be." So after many years being unhappy in office-based jobs, I strive to be the best gardener I can be.

'My dad left me with three pearls of wisdom,' he continues.

- 'A girl's best friend is her dad.
- Never trust a man who wears a hat whilst driving.
- If you have nothing nice to say, don't say anything at all.

'I'm not sure where they have got me in life,' he says, 'but if I am being quiet, it's probably best not to ask me what is wrong!! [Dad] also gave me my love of words, books, sport and family.'

Sage words from dad, I think, as I leave Mark to his veg and continue on my journey up the little lane. Once I'm through a wooden five-bar gate, the road converges with a dirt track and I'm suddenly walking under a canopy of woodland trees. After just a few minutes in the shade, I can feel the change in temperature; the cooler autumnal air is far more apparent in this tunnel of foliage. I catch glimpses of the rolling Downs blinking through the trees to my left as I walk up the track.

The reason I'm here is that I'm meeting successful author, James Lovegrove, under the trees. As I'm walking though, I notice a difference in Colin, our soundman from Cheshire, who isn't usually easily enthused. For him, the highlight of the day is the pint he has with Jan, our cameraman, at the end of a walk. When he isn't working, he says, 'I don't have any hobbies. I'm too lazy and I don't go anywhere nice or foreign unless I'm being paid to.' However, today I notice a definite flutter (or maybe just a 'flap') of excitement. You see our author, James, like Colin, has a lifelong obsession with the fictional character who's rather central to this part of the story.

Let me explain. Next to the walled garden sits another pretty cottage sporting a blue plaque on the wall, the kind I'm used to seeing all over London, where there are nearly 900 of them. Since 1866, English Heritage has been placing blue plaques on the exteriors of buildings in which famous people have lived and worked – like Oscar Wilde's home in Tite Street or Kenneth Williams' in Farley Court. But they are only found in London, so why am I currently looking at one, bearing the name of a *fictional* detective, on this cottage in East Dean?

'It's not a genuine blue plaque,' James explains. 'You may have noticed that. It's a gag; a nice gag, it treats the house as though Sherlock Holmes lived there, when he retired in about 1904.' And, indeed, the plaque states: 'Sherlock Holmes, consulting detective & bee keeper retired here 1903–1917'.

'It's all part of the fun of Sherlock Holmes,' continues James. 'There's a lot of people who believe that Sherlock Holmes is a real person. He's not. He's a made-up character in books. But there was a recent British survey, in which 21 per cent of the people who responded said that they thought he was a genuine, living existing person.'

In fairness to them, Holmes does live on in people's minds and hearts and people, like James, who also writes about him, support the mythology surrounding the detective.

'As a Sherlockian, part of the fun is treating him as a historical figure,' James admits, 'and getting all the biographical details right, making sure that whatever you write is in continuity with the existing canon of stories that [Sir Arthur] Conan Doyle wrote.' Although, as James points out, Sherlock Holmes' creator, Conan Doyle, got things wrong in the stories. 'Watson's injury sometimes moves from his shoulder to his leg; Watson is even called "James" in one of the stories instead of "John"; however, [Conan Doyle] did like to use real places in his books, to make them more authentic and gripping.'

209

While the whole plaque thing may be a joke (which tourists lap up), Sherlock Holmes and Sir Arthur Conan Doyle do have genuine connections to the area. In 'His Last Bow', Conan Doyle wrote that Holmes retired to 'a small farm upon the Downs, five miles from Eastbourne'. Also, the author stayed near by, James points out: 'at Birling Manor Farm, as a guest, nearby; he also lived in Sussex, in Crowborough, which is just a few miles away.' He is even thought to have visited East Dean village itself. And that's not all: Holmes retired to take up bee-keeping and the village, being sheltered, would have been a good spot for his hobby. After that though, any claims for 'evidence' become slightly more spurious, so James and I leave it at that.

On many of my walks around Britain, I've come across places that writers have made 'theirs' and I've touched upon some of them in this book. This doesn't *feel* like 'Conan Doyle' country, though. If you ask most people to picture Sherlock Holmes, it'll pretty much always be in London at his home in Baker Street, even though he travelled and stories were written about his exploits on Dartmoor and in Switzerland. Even so, this would be a good place to 'retire' to.

Before we leave, James kindly gives his latest novel, *Sherlock Holmes: The Stuff of Nightmares*, to Colin – who I think is going to body pop through sheer excitement.

And so, we get back on the trail, which leads us out of the woodland into an open field. It's such a gorgeous day and it's good to feel the warming sun on my back again. The grass is springy under boot and it's impossible to dodge the sheep poo which is in abundance on the Downs, as are the sheep which have grazed here for centuries. Just like in the Lake District, the landscape here has been shaped by them, as seen in the closely cropped grass. There's a sheep centre close by on a really lovely family-run working farm where you can see the largest private collection of sheep in the world apparently – fifty different breeds of them. And you can get involved at lambing time, too – they do a 'be a shepherd for the night experience' if you really want to get your hands dirty. The other reason for the short grass is the rabbits. Watch where you put your feet because you don't want to trip in a rabbit burrow and land face down in yet more poo. Particularly not if you're near a TV camera, because the bastards will keep filming.

As I walk towards the brow of the gentle slope, I catch my first proper glimpse of the Channel in the distance and the distinctive white chalk cliffs against the bright blue sky. There they are: the Seven Sisters. I up my pace, heading towards a bench where I can sit next to the imaginatively named 'Red Barn' (I don't need to explain what it looks like) and take in the view. It's inspiring: the light's gorgeous; the English Channel is glimmering. I think about the mischievous person who came up with the name for those lovely dips between the seven famous white cliffs, which are most often photographed from the sea. Mark The Gardener had prepared me for The

Bottoms, which include Short Bottom, Flathill Bottom and . . . Rough Bottom.

Time for my joke to camera: 'I think we're agreed – the Seven Sisters all have lovely bottoms . . . but their faces aren't bad either.'

Actually, the Seven Sisters are on their way to being eight now. Thanks to erosion of the cliff, a new sister is slowly being formed. Although this chalk was laid down 65 million years ago, it was actually 10,000 years ago – when the English Channel burst through to separate England from France after the Ice Age – that the chalk cliffs were revealed to the world. Since then, they've taken on an almost mythic significance. While it might be Dover's white cliffs that get sung about, the Seven Sisters feature not only in our island's history, but are shown in numerous films as a symbol of England, from *Robin Hood: Prince of Thieves* to *Atonement*. Maybe that's because they really are white here, whereas in Dover, with a port in front of them, they have a slightly greenish tinge. Doesn't sound so good, does it? 'The slightly green Cliffs of Dover'.

I soak up the view while I sip some water. We've lucked out with the weather. A butterfly flutters about my feet and prompts me to think about this beautiful chalk grassland that is so special and that harbours such a fragile ecosystem. These grassy downlands are home to a mind-boggling array of plants and little creatures. The small wildflower horseshoe vetch *only* grows here because the sheep graze away the long grass that would otherwise compete for its vital nutrients and sun, and without horseshoe vetch there wouldn't be the brilliantly coloured Adonis blue butterfly. The caterpillars *only* feed on the nectar of that plant and lay their eggs under its leaves. The Adonis blue also relies on the presence of ants, which feast on the honey-like substance produced by the caterpillars and pupae, as the ants protect this substance because they love it so much. If the grass is too long (back to the sheep), the sun won't warm the anthills and the ants will vamoose, so with no protection from parasites and predators, no Adonis blue . . . it's these complex networks that need protecting and appreciating. Alarmingly we've lost 80 per cent of grasslands like these across the country.

They're working hard to reverse this process in the South Downs National Park by clearing away invasive scrub and propagating local grassland seeds. This work is obviously beneficial to bucketloads of other plants and animal species. Sometimes people are sceptical about projects like this but I've probably heard about more than most through my filming experiences and I know that things can be reversed with passion and perseverance. They've already seen the unexpected return here of the silver-spotted skipper butterfly which has been on the edge of extinction across the country. Species and flora and fauna near extinction can make comebacks if we're devoted enough.

A good little weather tip here: look at what's going on on the ground around you. Insects don't like the rain, so if you can't see any when you look down, there's a good chance rain is on the way. It's the same with butterflies and bees. If they flit away, here comes the rain again. Alas, not falling on my head like a memory (Annie Lennox got it wrong).

Left to his devices, Jan would stay here for hours. 'Come on, Janusz,' I call, using his full Polish name. 'Let's get cracking.'

'Just one more shot. It looks bloody lovely.' He leans over his big camera, left eye up close to viewfinder while his stout dextrous fingers adjust the lens to the scene in front of us.

'Janusz – we've got to split. Last one . . .'

He carries on.

It was near here that a famous wartime patriotic poster emerged, urging people to fight for their country. Against the backdrop of this very view of the Downs, a shepherd, his dog and his flock in the foreground, were the words, 'Your Britain: Fight For It Now', a simple but strong message. The artist was Frank Newbould and the poster appeared in 1942, when things must have seemed pretty bleak to the British people. Yes, the Battle of Britain was over and the threat of invasion lifted and, yes, America had joined the war effort, but the country had still endured three hard years of bombing, rationing, setbacks abroad in the Far East and the day-to-day drudgery and misery of thinking that the war might never end. It's easy for us now to see the Big Picture, but it was only towards the *end* of 1942 that Winston Churchill made his famous speech, stating 'this is not the end. It is not even the beginning of the end. But it is, perhaps, the end of the beginning' – so Newbould's poster was produced when people were still pretty desperate and times were hard. Newbould produced other posters, which are still incredibly popular. Standing here, well over seventy years later though, I can well understand why that particular image, the timeless nature of the shepherd's occupation, evoking an idyllic picture of the Downs, was so very appealing at the time. Spurred on, I make my way towards the crest of the hill and go through the kissing-gate at the top.

Because we're only filming with one camera, we have to redo the shot of me walking through the kissing-gate a few times – once from behind, once from the front, then a close-up of my hand on the latch. All these shots then get stitched together in the edit so that my walk through the gate flows naturally on screen and you can see it from different angles. Ah, the sorcery of telly. Anyway, while we're doing this, I can see a couple toiling up the hill towards us. They're both watching with curiosity my multiple attempts to walk through a gate. As they draw closer, I notice the woman, who's wearing sunglasses and a black cap, is looking with interest at the cameras and at me.

'Oh, yes, I recognize you,' says actress Gina McKee at exactly the same time as I recognize her, then off she goes, carrying on over the hill. As I've said, walking is a great leveller and you meet all kinds of people along the way.

I'm aiming to reach the Birling Gap on the next stretch of the walk so that I can get down on to the beach and look up at the eroding cliffs. On the way down, I pass banks of dense yellow gorse bushes. If you can bear to stick your nose in to them, you may smell the scent of coconut. Weirdly some people smell it very strongly and others can barely smell it all. It seems to depend on the nose, the nasal receptors actually. I've got a big nose so it's Pina Colada heaven to me. There are hundreds of heavenly flowers and plants across the Downs, but wherever you are in the country there's almost always some gorse in flower, because there are so many species. Hence the country saying: 'When gorse is out of blossom, kissing's out of fashion.'

Walking on the Downs reminds me of the time when I was filming *The Great British Countryside* with the lovely and extremely talented Hugh Dennis of the hilarious comedy *Outnumbered* and *Mock the Week*, among others. Hugh is good company, as you can imagine, full of amusing stories and anecdotes. He made me laugh, telling me about the countryside walks he used to do with his family when he was younger. His father was an Anglican bishop, his mother a school teacher and they'd all come here to the South Downs on family holidays . . . with the family cat leading the way, on a washing line. 'At times,' Hugh said, 'my father would walk into a village shop with the cat wrapped around his shoulders, like a stole. It all seemed perfectly normal at the time.' Indeed. While Hugh was making me laugh with his funny anecdotes I was making him laugh with my breast-feeding antics. I'd had my son 12 weeks earlier who was on the road with me, and this meant lots of inconvenient 'comfort breaks' from filming - mostly in pub car parks. He was very patient.

I get down to the famous Birling Gap pebble beach on the ugly but practical galvanized steel staircase (the steps have been victims of coastal erosion too and have been replaced again and again) and inhale the sea air. I watch, interested, as a man heads down after me carrying a James Bond-style metal case, which I recognize as a kit bag. He drops to his knees, clicks open the locks with each thumb and lo-and-behold he starts pulling out bits of machinery which he fits together to make up a drone. I don't mean a male bee, wasp or ant. I mean an UAV – an unmanned aerial vehicle. They're incredibly popular now and scarily *anyone* can fly them. We use them a lot in telly, with a camera attached, to film aerial shots (far cheaper than a helicopter), but they can be difficult to control and temperamental. If you don't know what you're doing or the batteries fail, they can drop out of the sky like a dead bird. Mr Bond assembles his toy and proceeds to fly it up and down the chalky cliffs. I hope there are no nudists on the beach today or they may get caught on film from above (they tend to hang out on the west side of the beach, turn right at the bottom of the steps).

Because the Birling Gap is an access point to the sea on the south coast, it's been used and fought over by all the invaders of England, from the Romans through to the Vikings and the Normans. There's evidence that people lived here during the Bronze Age, about 4,000 years ago, but since then erosion has shifted the cliffs back almost 4km (2 miles). These beautiful white chalky cliffs erode almost a metre each year. That's a pretty shocking statistic for those people living nearby and all the holiday makers who visit every year, too. There have been coastguard cottages here since the nineteenth century. I have some photos with me, showing ten cottages lined up. Now there are only four left. It's extraordinary to see how dramatic the change is in no time at all. This is history in action, watching the landscape retreat in front of our eyes.

Back at the top of the stairs I stop for a coffee in the National Trust café which used to be a posh hotel; now it's used not only to feed thousands of tourists, but also to house the memories of those who grew up in those cottages. It seems the area still has the pulling power it held over the Victorians when it was a popular location, but the reckoning is that are only another ten years or so left for the café before it, too, is swallowed up by the Channel. Raven-haired Natasha Sharma from the NT has assembled the exhibition recording these memories. She's passionate about what she does and takes some time out to tell me a bit about the history.

'People have been coming here for years,' she comments.

'They have their memories of their holidays, staying in the cottages, the hotel, or camping. One of the clubs that came down to camp every year was a Boys' Club from south-east London called Hollington. They brought boys here who wouldn't have had the opportunity for a holiday otherwise.' Hollington was opened by Dulwich College as a club 'for the benefit of fatherless boys', over 120 years ago, and the boys came here up until the 1960s. Natasha continues, 'Many of them return and tell me how much fun they had back then – and they're now in their seventies. They used to climb the flagpole as a challenge and there was a big rock out at sea they'd swim up to and then dive off. People still do that today.'

During the Second World War, because of the threat of invasion, the beach became part of the nation's defence operation and was barred from public access, but that didn't deter everyone.

'All the sneaky little children, who managed to wheedle their way onto here, have memories of coming to find what the troops were up to,' laughs Natasha.

I suppose things have changed since then. Natasha tells me that they still get lots of local visitors, coming to picnic and enjoy the privacy that the beach entails. 'It's away from most of the crowds [and] you can always pick a time when you'll be alone on the beach, especially when the tide's out,' she comments.

The National Trust has a lot to say about life on our coastline – they look after over 1,240km (over 770 miles) of it – how fragile it is and what we need to do not only to protect it, but also to cherish it. 'Action is now needed by all coastal stake-holders to manage the threats to our beautiful and diverse coast to prevent us drifting into a future where our coast is a rim of concrete,' warns the NT.

Birling Gap is certainly the place that reminds you how lucky we are to have such a relatively intact coastline – 74 per cent of the coast in England, Wales and Northern Ireland remains unspoilt. You can swim here, surf, go rock pooling and hunt fossils. I used to love combing the long sandy beaches in Scotland with my mum and dad when I was a little girl. We used to stay at a friend's house in the village of Rhu on Gare Loch in Argyll and Bute and every day we'd spend hours exploring the sands when the tide was out. I remember being very excited when we found a distressed catfish, stranded. I spent hours splashing water over its gills until we could release it back into the water. I think I wanted to be a vet that summer. I was about seven.

I thank Natasha and continue on my way, walking away from the cliffs in search of a different mood. As I head downhill, I pass the Belle Tout Lighthouse again on my right, but it's not the end of this hike yet, as I'm on my way to find another 'Bottom' – Wigden's, this time, a little haven of peace and tranquillity. This shallow valley offers ideal shelter from salty sea winds. The ancient tribes of Sussex often used to bury their ancestors in these basins so there are several burial mounds around here. I take a moment to stop and absorb the scenery – the now undulating green hills, the sloping dips of grassy green rolling out in front of me. The air is rich with the scent of wild thyme; delicate flower heads nod in the breeze.

'How uniquely British,' I think.

I look hopefully at the flower heads, but it's too late in the year to see any orchids and besides which Orchid Hunting is an art. That said, nearly half of the orchid species native to Britain (and there are round fifty) are native to the grasslands and woodlands of the South Downs. In fact, it wasn't far from here that I had the most amazing experience with David Lang, an internationally reknowned orchid expert when he witnessed something that he'd never seen in over forty years – a wasp pollinating a fly orchid. We managed to capture the whole thing on camera – that is the joy of filmmaking, capturing moments like this for ever. You could never guarantee finding a fly orchid, let alone seeing this extraordinary event happen in front of your eyes. Each flower looks like a slim green-and-brown-black fly, but it's meant to replicate a small female wasp in order to attract a male. The orchid's pollen then sticks to the head of the male wasp which carries it from plant to plant in an attempt to mate. So it's a flower pretending to be an insect. Nature is so frigging clever.

I now have two goals: first, to reach the famous chalk headland of Beachy Head and then, of course, the gorgeous

Belle Tout Lighthouse, a lovely beacon on top of the cliff. Leaving the valley, the sun is setting and that familiar golden glow is diffusing across the skies. I come across someone else taking advantage of the beauty and peacefulness, Jackie Wrigglesworth. She's one of those people who seem to fill their life with so much activity that it puts the rest of us to shame. She's here because she's teaching a yoga class nearby, but that's not the half of what she does. A Fellow of the Royal Geographical Society, she also leads expeditions around the world and, back before we knew who Angelina Jolie was, Jackie was flown to Hollywood to be considered for the role of Lara Croft in the first *Tomb Raider* movie.

Jackie is a very exotic-looking woman (her mother is Venezuelan). She has been to more than seventy countries around the world and she's younger than me. I ask her what it is that she likes about travelling.

'It keeps life constantly exciting and interesting,' she says. 'You're always discovering new things, places and people. Travelling is a constant feast for the senses.'

When she is in another country, Jackie takes on a project. She's involved with lots of charities and sustainable development projects in Mexico and the Amazon; building language schools; and has even harvested rainwater in Fiji. One of her favourite community projects is The Book Bus, which takes books to children who otherwise wouldn't have access to them in Zambia, Malawi, Ecuador and India. They also operate at home in the UK. In addition, Jackie sits on the fundraising committee for the British Red Cross.

Jackie's yoga is a large part of her life and she has practised all over the world. She is, as you might imagine, incredibly fit and looks superbly flexible. It's all a bit intimidating, frankly. I do yoga a few times a year; Jackie definitely does it every day.

'Right, shall we have a yogi moment before I go?' I ask her.

'Why not? Let's take in the energy of this beautiful sun,' she replies.

We both sit in the crossed legs position, looking out over the heavenly scene, hands upturned on our knees. The waves of the sparkling English Channel are dipping in agreement with the surging hills. Jackie initiates a mini meditation session.

'Something I was taught many years ago; while you're breathing, sitting here, tune into a favourite memory of your life and relive it in your mind, over and over. It's called the Bliss Meditation.' We both close our eyes and feel the sun and evening sea breeze on our faces. It's amazing how just a few minutes of calm and reflection in nature can soothe you and recharge the brain.

As I hike up a grassy slope for my final stretch of the walk, the sound of the birds and the distant waves seem amplified after my moment with Jackie. 'It's been a good detour – a real adventure,' she says about her life and that could equally stand for our brief encounter. It's a reminder of how things weave and whirl along and then can change direction in the blink of an eye because of one conversation, encounter or a single decision that someone else makes. It's somehow appropriate that I'm thinking this as I approach the brow of the hill where I can see Beachy Head rising up in front of me.

The highest chalk cliff by the sea in England, Beachy Head sits over 160m (530ft) above sea level. It's a popular location and scenes from children's films *Harry Potter and the Goblet of Fire* and the iconic *Chitty Chitty Bang Bang*, when the car of the title plunges over the edge of the cliff and then flies, were filmed here. *Chitty Chitty Bang Bang* was also written by Ian Fleming, author of the James Bond novels, and the climax of the opening sequence of *The Living Daylights*, supposedly set in Gibraltar, was filmed here, as was David Bowie's video for 'Ashes to Ashes'. I could go on. And I haven't even mentioned Jane Austen (the South Downs connection, generally).

Sadly though, Beachy Head is well-known for another reason. When I arrived, I took a photograph in the Beachy Head car park of the ticket machine because it has a little sticker on it with a phone number for The Samaritans. Beachy Head is a notorious suicide spot, at which about twenty people a year choose to take their lives. This is an issue about which I'm going to be talking to artist and hairdresser, Nathan Burr.

A hip, bearded man in his thirties, Nathan is from nearby Brighton. He set up a project with Louise Buckley called A

100-Mile Conversation (suicidewatch.net) in response to the number of suicides at Beachy Head, involving getting people out and about, walking. I ask Nathan how he came up with the idea for the project and he tells me the seed was planted when he went through some personal difficulties and decided to go for a walk, which took him up to the South Downs Way and on to Winchester. About two days in, he said, he realized that 'the sky was blue, the sun was shining and my spirits had lifted. Walking had had a really dramatic effect on my mood.

'It got me thinking about the landscape and if that could be used; if I was walking in the opposite direction, towards Beachy Head, with its connotations as a notorious suicide spot, what could have happened to me?'

'God. If you'd have walked in the other direction when you first set out, in that mood, and arrived at Beachy Head at just the wrong time—?' I say out loud.

'Exactly. But I did walk the other way so I had that distance away from it and I started thinking, could it be used as a therapeutic space? The 100-mile walk project began as a place to meet a series of experts with different perspectives on end-of-life issues: archaeologists, sociologists, Samaritans – people with personal experiences of suicide, all at different locations on the walk. So the conversations would also be about ancient burial mounds and how Neolithic people would have buried suicides – so it was all connected to the landscape. Over the nine-day walk, as we neared Beachy Head, other people joined and at the end we had twenty-five of us involved. It ended on a positive note, with my nan's cakes for us all!'

It's not what you'd call a traditional guided walk, but I think it's brilliant. There's actually a similar successful project in the United States, promoting community action to prevent suicides by getting people to walk outdoors.

'I am talking about the landscape,' Nathan continues, 'about looking at how life and death is contained within it. It's about being alive and creating social bonds between people but while we're also talking about this other side of life – death.'

And now he's made a film of the walk, as a way of opening the conversation up to those it's aimed at. 'Walking is conducive to being open. You're not being formal or in a conflicting position to have a conversation,' Nathan tells me. 'You've got the ups and the downs and the weather, so it's easier to talk about suicide and other end-of-life issues.'

It's a serious subject to contemplate and I think it's great that Nathan has found a way of approaching such a difficult subject. We all find it tricky to talk about death and suicide statistics are shocking: in 2013, over 6,200 people killed themselves in the UK. In 2014, twelve men a day killed themselves – that's one every two hours. Suicide is the single biggest killer of men under 45 in the UK. Quite staggering, when you think of it like that. TheCALMzone.net (Campaign Against Living Miserably) is an active website that also addresses these issue and encourages conversation. Its strapline is: 'Let's talk #biggerissues.'

The interesting thing is when we got the filming permit from Eastbourne council to film at Beachy Head, there was a line stipulating that we wouldn't, under any circumstances, mention suicide. Imagine that. That's not exactly 'having a conversation', is it?

Nathan and I are walking up the final stretch of cliff towards Belle Tout now. At last, after so many sightings along the way, it's within spitting distance. Nathan peels off the grassy path and leaves me to savour the last leg on my own. 'Mind the edge,' he jokes.

This squat lighthouse, built in 1832, is perched proudly on the promontory of Beachy Head. It might sound French, but the name is actually Celtic and means 'war look-out'. There was an Iron Age fort here thousands of years ago and various forms of lighthouses have been built over the centuries to watch out for smugglers, as well as protect the ships from the fog. Not all the smugglers were of the friendly East Dean village variety, some of them were quite unscrupulous would you believe. In the early part of the eighteenth century, we're told they tied lanterns to animals that would then move about, mimicking the movement of ships afloat in the water. Unwary sailors would steer their boats onto the rocks, thinking they must be heading towards safe waters if other boats were sailing there. The pirates would pounce and steal their cargo. Sneaky.

Sadly there was a flaw with Belle Tout and it was decom-missioned because of the constant clifftop fog that hindered its effectiveness and also because of the retreating cliffs. The Beachy Head Lighthouse, built down on the actual beach, replaced it in 1902. Since then it's been through a lot, having been a tearoom, a private residence, and almost completely destroyed during the Second World War; it's been the home of a she-devil (in the BBC's *The Life and Loves of a She-Devil*) and now it's a rather special B&B. What a life. As if that wasn't eventful enough, in 1999 a complex engineering feat saw the entire structure move 17m (56ft) back from the lip of the cliff, using greased steel-topped concrete beams, as the threat of erosion edged ever closer. It cost £250,000 and has been set up so that should they need to move it again, they can. The Belle Tout is a very unique landmark. I wouldn't call it pretty, but it's certainly striking and it surely must be the world's first – perhaps only – movable lighthouse? By all accounts it's a stunning pad. I wave up at some guests staring down at me from the lighthouse's lantern room. It's encircled by a balcony and must offer 360-degree views over the cliffs, the sea and the rolling hills.

'I hope none of you are sleepwalkers!' I shout out. They're too high up to hear me, but they wave back, clearly thinking, 'Who's that crazy bint down there? Don't let her in.'

It's an obscenely gorgeous location on which to finish my walk today. By the coast, the extraordinary beauty of the land-scape, the green rolling hills, the white chalk face, the bluey-grey English Channel, are all complemented by a fabulous evening sky – what I can only describe as 'Big Sky'. Long trailing clouds move through the yellowy-orange space, drifting slowly down to the horizon. It's glorious, and it's a great moment for me to reflect on today. On the people I have met, like Jackie, who travel the world but have this beauty on their doorstep; Nathan, who wants to use this fabulous setting to reconnect people's lives; and Mark Proctor, whose living depends upon the very gifts that the seasons bestow, the rain and the sun, on days like this. And also, on the millions of people who've been here before me, from all walks of life.

An old yoga mantra comes to mind, 'salute the sun and take in the light, warmth and energy'. Big Sky, Big Thoughts. Makes sense. So, what are mine? How long will it take me to get home to cuddle my babies. And what will we have for supper?

WALKER'S GUIDE:
WHERE TO STAY, WHERE TO EAT,
WHAT TO SEE, WHAT TO DO

To start: I began at the Tiger Inn (The Green, East Dean BN20 0DA), and I reckon you should too.

To see: The Sherlock Holmes plaque in East Dean, where – it is supposed – the great detective retired to keep bees (http://www.beachyhead.org.uk/latest/2012/01/did-sherlock-holmes-retire-near-beachy-head/).

To pause: The National Trust Café at the Birling Gap is an excellent place to break the walk and have a coffee in stunning surroundings.

To stay: The Grand Hotel (King Edwards Paradem, Eastbourne BN21 4EQ – https://curatedby.theoutdoorguide.co.uk/grandeastbournehotel) more than lives up to its name!

To see or stay: The Belle Tout Lighthouse is on this walk: no longer a working lighthouse but now a completely unique B&B. Worth a look even if you can't get a room (Beauley Head BN20 0AE – http://www.belletout.co.uk/).

8

PEAK DISTRICT: THE KINDER SCOUT WALK

'Be free'

The Dale folds down
In its shadow stir seeds
Of childhood memories
– A haiku by Michael Bradbury, October 2015

This chapter is something of a love letter to a part of the world I was introduced to by my father and it's somewhere that will always be very special to me because it was where I first came to love walking in the hills.

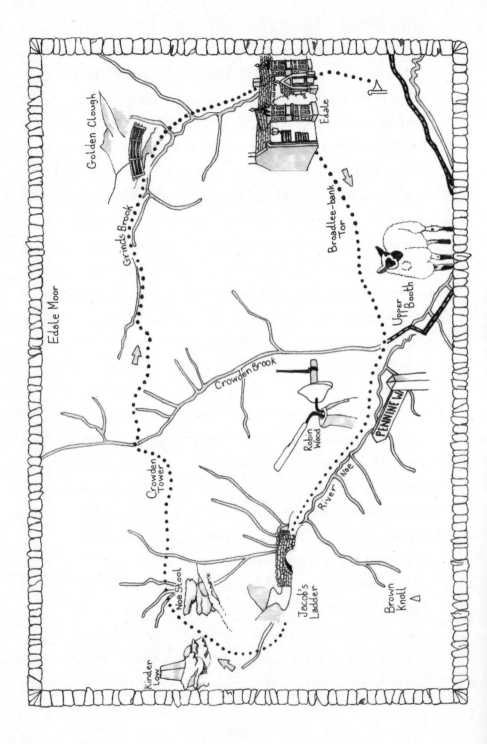

So, first off, a huge thank-you, dad (that's Michael, the author of the lovely haiku), for dragging an (at first) unwilling child out on all those walks, for introducing me to the Great British Countryside and the joys of striding out on the hills and tracks and for . . . well, just being my dad, really. As he hasn't been well recently (following a health scare involving my mum), this walk is especially emotional for me because he joins me on it, so I'm savouring every moment that I can.

We all have places where we can picture our family, our mums and dads, our siblings. For some people, it might be seeing their mum or dad at home, reading the paper, pottering in the garden; for others, it might be someone on holiday, in the sunshine. For me, if I think of my mum, Chrissi, I see her in her shop, chatting to customers, holding swathes of fabric up to them, designing shapes and styles; my sister Gina is always in her office, telephone clamped to her ear, laughing raucously at something the caller's just said. My dad, though, I see out in the open, here on the edge of the Peak District, hands crammed into his battered old Barbour jacket (that has long since lost any weatherproofness), his face alive with the pleasure of being in the fresh air, rain or shine.

I'm meeting mum and dad at The Old Nag's Head in the village of Edale, in Derbyshire, and I arrive just in time for lunch. Perfect. My parents have driven over from Rutland and the crew arrived earlier this morning after a couple of welcome days at home. There's nothing like your own bed.

'Hello my chuckle,' my dad says. 'How are the babies?'

'All good thanks, Daddio. It was hard to leave them this morning,' I admit, as I lean in to give them both a hug and a kiss.

The plan today is to start the walk right outside the pub at the beginning of the Pennine Way and then we'll head up a gentle slope to a good-looking spot where dad and I can 'have a chat'. He's in his seventies now with bad knees (all that walking!) and the days of doing long hikes together have passed us by, which is sad. I'll never get to a summit again with my dad or a cliff edge, where we can share the view and eat the last of the furry wine gums rescued from our pockets. Outside the pub, I look around me. There's something about this place that I adore; perhaps it's the greeny camouflage mix of the moor or the air. Living in London, I'm acutely aware of the 'smell' of fresh air when I'm on my walks and there's just a particular something about the Peak District air that I adore, maybe it's the way it filters through the rocks or something.

The Pennine Way is a 412km (256 miles) long National Trail that follows 'the backbone of Britain', the Pennine hills, all the way up to Kirk Yetholm, a village in the Scottish Borders. The trail was first proposed in 1935, but it wasn't until 1965 that the final section was completed. It was Britain's first National Trail and now there are fifteen across England and Wales, including the South Downs Way. The British Army were the first people to walk the Trail, checking the signage and so on – and the group completed it in one day. Not, I hasten to add, in one go, but by breaking the walk into 24km (15 miles) sections, which were covered by different teams. These days, if anyone attempts to walk it in one go (and most people don't, choosing to cover it in stages over weeks, months and even years), it would take them about three weeks. That said, I'm going to meet someone later who completed it in a much shorter space of time and I've already met Mike Hartley who ran (*ran!*) the Pennine Way in two days, seventeen hours and twenty minutes!

A walker now following the Pennine Way would have to cross 287 gates, 183 stone stiles, 249 wooden stiles, and 204 bridges to reach their destination and this is not to everyone's taste. My mate, Alfred Wainwright, for example, didn't enjoy his experience of the walk. I'd go so far as to say he hated it. At the end of his own *Pennine Way Companion* (Wainwright's book of the route, originally published in 1968), he wrote: 'you won't come across me anywhere along the Pennine Way. I've had enough of it.' He even offered to buy anyone who completed it a half-pint of beer; it's thought that this gesture cost him about fifteen grand by the end of his life. In contrast, the Yorkshire bard Ian McMillan wrote:

> *The Pennine Way is a beautiful thing*
> *In summer, autumn, winter, spring.*
> *As the clouds dance across the Pennine sky*
> *And the wild birds wheel past the walker's eye.*

I'm not attempting the full-length of the Trail today, just 8km (5 miles), but if you are considering doing so, the reason you start here – in The Old Nag's Head pub – is because you will be issued with a certificate that you can have stamped at the start and also at the finish to prove you have walked the full length of the Way. I am here, not just to meet my parents, but also because we're filming the bit where they stamp my certificate. It makes for a good beginning to this episode – but I won't be cheating, I promise. No final stamp for me.

This lovely pub, which has been standing here since 1577, is obviously popular with walkers and you'd probably be unpopular here these days if you *didn't* turn up in muddy boots and a wet cagoule. In the past, it was also a convenient stopping point on two significant old packhorse routes (packhorses were the only way to transport goods before a proper road network developed). It would have provided an overnight break for packhorsemen and their horses, as it not only had accommodation, but also a smithy, as well. Today the pub is alive with noisy groups though, all getting ready to set off, so it's time to crack on. I have a date with a very important man – my dad.

It's estimated that 50,000 people walk the Pennine Way every year, but only one per cent do it all in one three-week stint (they fit into the 'extremely keen/mad' category), so I'm very happy to show you here how a gorgeous three-hour walk can politely showcase some of the thrills of the Pennine Way, without the pain of the entire route. I'm definitely not saying don't have a go at the whole thing, but just don't blame me if you do.

Just up the road from The Old Nags Head, I walk through a small oak gate which has the Pennine Way route intricately carved into the middle panel; just another *aide memoire*, in case you need it, that this is the Big One in terms of walks. The gate was put in to mark the fiftieth anniversary of this epic route that was the idea of outdoor writer Tom Stephenson. He first proposed the Pennine Way in 1935 when he realized that walkers in the United States had routes like the Appalachian trail, but there was no equivalent here in the UK.

I push through the gate and set off on the first gentle stretch uphill. I have filmed with my dad before a few times around the Peaks. In fact, the last time we were here we remarked on the weather, it was bloody gorgeous. 'I haven't seen a day like this in the Peak District for about fourteen years,' my dad said then. Well, someone up there is playing a blinder because today might possibly be even more delicious, for which I'm glad.

Taking a deep breath, I look around me, taking in all the different colours of green that sway and rustle in the wind. This is the northern Dark Peak, so the geology is gritstone, as opposed to the southern White Peak which is mainly limestone. Climbers love the area and there are numerous routes all over the Peaks, none more famous than Stanage Edge, about 16km (10 miles) from Edale. It's a gritstone escarpment that has over 400 routes described across it.

The geology of an area obviously has an impact on the fauna and flora and when you're up on these moors you can expect to see all sorts of lovely things from pretty bilberry shrubs, purple honey-scented heather and bog asphodel, to hare's-tail cottongrass (imagine loads of tiny afghan hounds with their heads stuck out of the car window). A few tufts float by as I make my way up the track.

The Edale Valley is peppered with 'booths'. The name belongs to the former little shelters in which a farmer could take shelter in bad weather, when out minding his herds. There's Lady Booth, Barber Booth and Grindsbrook Booth (which is where Edale village itself is), among others, but I'm on my way along a pretty little track up towards Upper Booth. Waiting on the side of the path, sitting in the sunshine on a fallen tree, is my dad and it's here we'll have our 'chat'. There's a lot to talk about: Kinder Scout and what happened there, why it's so important in the history of walking in Great Britain, this craggy unique landscape, Yorkshiremen vs Derbyshire men But what I really want to talk about is our days together here as father and daughter, not least because I'm thinking of bringing my own little brood up here one day, to experience it as I did those few short years ago.

'This is where you started your walking,' says dad. 'Not right here, but not far away.'

I was six years old when dad first brought me up here with him for a walk. I can't recall much, if anything, of that first time, of course, but I do remember both of us perched on the back bumper of his car, me tying up the laces of my new brown hiking boots which dad had bought me. I was so excited.

'Was I was always a great walker?' I ask him jokily.

'You were a great walker in one sense, but an awkward walker in another,' he comments.

Awkward – me? What can he possibly mean?

'You were a little escapologist,' he explains. 'You'd try and run away. Apart from that, you were okay.'

'You always found me,' I say.

'Yes, I always did . . . Forty years later, I'm still regretting it,' he chuckles. I'm suddenly reminded that he can say anything and probably will. He's not shy, my dad. When I interviewed him for my *Railway Walks* series, years ago, he let slip a little belter about our trout tickling experiences not far from here, near Buxton.

'Ah yes, you never forget your first fish; it's a bit like your first woman. Slippery to touch and . . .'

'*Dad!*' I yelled.

My father was born and brought up about 17 km (11 miles) south of here, in Tideswell. He used to walk in the area around there – Monks Dale was a particular favourite and he describes it as 'atmospheric, very narrow, very rough stones, absolutely magical'. Dad is a very proud Derbyshire man, explaining that the county, because of its situation on the Pennines, combines the best of Lancashire and the best of Yorkshire ('we arbitrate between them, and leave the rotten stuff to them').

Dad's a tall fella (1.9m/6ft 5in) with a twinkle in his eye and he tells a good tale. One TV critic described him as a 'bit of a Swiss Tony', after the Charlie Higson car dealer character from *The Fast Show*. That couldn't be further from the truth, though. He is lovely, kind, ridiculously knowledgeable about all sorts of things, but he is definitely not 'smooth' and he couldn't sell a secondhand car. I tell you one thing, I think my dad has taken on at least one Yorkshire trait and made it very much his own: he has a severe case of what we call 'crocodile pockets', that is, his pockets on occasion grow sharp snappy crocodile teeth that prevent his arms from reaching his wallet.

Dad's used to walking in all seasons and claims it's the infamous Peaks weather that makes the people of the area who they are: 'This kind of variable weather hardens you, toughens you,' he says. 'It also makes you grateful for small mercies – a gleam of sun for five minutes in the morning can lighten up the whole day. Then the rains come in and you get wet.'

The walks he took me on as a child do, like so many childhood memories, blend into one. I do remember coming up on to the moors as a small child in winter and being dwarfed by the snowdrifts that towered above me. We dug out massive tunnels together; he showed me how to make an igloo and, of course, we had snowball fights. A lot of our childhood memories, those we can recall clearly anyway, play tricks on us – things that were vast, but when seen again as an adult are just ordinary sized, that kind of thing. The drifts on the Peaks were real though. I read about them a winter or two ago: people were snowed in for days on end as drifts reached heights of up to 6m (20ft). Hmm – I think I'll stick to the spring, summer or autumn days to walk here with my little ones. I don't think they're ready for that yet.

When my dad first started walking here, the moorland and hills wouldn't have been as busy as they are today. Now, he says, 'millions of people come up here, every year, as an escape from the stresses and strains of modern life'.

We're sitting in a tree in front of a bench (why are we sitting in a tree, I hear you ask, when we could be sitting on a bench? Er. Because it's in the sunshine, of course). It has a wonderful poem etched into the seat that encapsulates some of what dad's just said.

Office bustle for leaves rustle. Mobiles ringing for birds singing. Lover's rejection for water's reflection. Twenty-first Century for glimpse of eternity.

This was written by Lynne Rowbottom, one of a group of locals who won a competition to have their poems inscribed on benches across the Peak District.

As memorials go, it's better than those benches that have little plaques on them. This small bench is charming and it's a testament to what awaits me up ahead, on the top of Kinder Scout. It's an amazing thing, I think to myself, how those childhood memories of walking really do stick with you. If, as a youngster, you have experiences in the great outdoors in brilliant national parks like this one (our first ever national park, let's not forget), when you grow up and become an adult you relish that chance to get out there again, to escape the complexities of life, its schedules, its arrangements and meetings. Walking becomes an escape to freedom. I've got my dad to thank for all of that. And it is free, as well. But my time with my dad has come to an end. I give him a big hug, wishing that he could do the whole walk with me.

As I follow the gritty track of the Pennine Way that's been carved by millions of walking boots, on my left are fields, while on my right I can see the steep slopes leading to the high moors on top. The place closest to me is called Broadlee Bank Tor; the green grass at the base fades slowly to a dry brown at the top, mottled with patches of heathers. There's a little morning mist hanging around and it drifts about the hillsides, tantalizing me with the occasional glimpse of the climb to come. I stop and take a moment to see if I can spot any wildlife. In front of me, a patchwork of green fields, dotted with brushy trees and textured by different grasses and heather, roll on and on. Huge mounds frame either side of the valley and loom in the distance. It's as if some giant has taken the land and shaken it up, like a duvet, with flat places and rising edges.

I'm no professional twitcher, but I know this is a good place to see all sorts of bird life, from merlins to short-eared owls. There's nothing though, as I scour the skies above . . . and then, in the distance, I see a red grouse flap out of some long undergrowth, disturbed by something. You see red grouse here all year round.

I'm only just getting started and the valley is opening up in front of me. I can't see the toughest section of the walk from here, but I know it's waiting: Jacob's Ladder. But before I get to Jacob, I'm going to meet up with a shepherdess called Alice Helliwell at Upper Booth Farm – a cluster of buildings up ahead. What would this chapter be if I didn't meet up with a shepherdess? It would be like a chapter of Harry Potter without the wizardry. Upper Booth is a family run farm, part of the National Trust's High Peak Estate.

Alice is in her early twenties and is absolutely brimming with cheerfulness. I start by asking her about the Mule ewe lambs in the field in front of us. She tells me that they've been sold and 'will be going to their new house in a week or so'. It's a sign of the way Alice thinks about the animals on the farm, the cattle and the sheep. She's concerned about where they live and she genuinely cares for them. Still, I imagine them packing up their belongings and loading them into the removal van.

Alice's sister also works in farming in the Cotswolds, actually on my old friend from *Countryfile* Adam Henson's farm, no less.

'I hope he's looking after her,' I joke.

'Oh yes, she's loving it,' Alice says. I ask her why the two of them don't go into business. That would be unique – two sisters running a farm together.

'Mmm. We've never really talked about it,' Alice says, pondering the thought.

She has worked on other farms, mainly with sheep, but, contrary to some of the other shepherdesses I've spoken to, like Rosie, in the Lake District or my friend Amanda Owen, Alice's experiences of working as a woman on a farm have been completely positive.

'Most of [the farmers] are used to it – around here there's a fair few shepherdesses. Most of them have got daughters of their own – [so it's] no different really.' Alice thinks it's the public rather than the farmers who tend to be surprised by the notion of shepherdesses. 'When they see you walking around and you've got nail varnish on, you get a few comments,' she says.

'But you're allowed to look pretty when working!' I exclaim.

Alice's four-year-old Collie, Moss, is now looking longingly up at her mistress, waiting for her next instruction. 'She's a good working dog when she listens properly,' Alice comments, 'although sometimes she's a bit speedy'.

I love visiting the Peaks, and on days like today they are world beating, but I'm not sure I'd cut it here being out in all weathers, herding livestock around. It seems to suit Alice though.

'You can't get any better than these views,' she says. 'I grew up with it; it's what I know. I've seen these lambs grow up; I know they've had a perfect life – [you] couldn't make it any better for them.'

Her passion for what she does is obvious. 'That's the reason

I do it, really – looking after them [the animals], working with them.'

I know some people find it odd that a farmer can be this close to her flock and then choose to sell the sheep off for meat, but it's not a problem for Alice. She sees the whole process from rearing an animal, right through to taking it to market – and she really does see the 'whole process' because she also works at a local auctioneer's, doing the paperwork on the livestock that are sold there. Some times of year are busier than others, 'depending on the religious feasts and things', she says. Only the week before we meet, Alice dealt with over 4,000 sheep sales. 'That's a lot of paperwork!' I say. But doing the paperwork ensures she makes everything run smoothly at the farm, so the end result is an easier life for both her and the family.

The Pennine Way passes right through Alice's family farm and the tourists who come in such large numbers are always fascinated by her job as a shepherdess, often standing and watching while she's working in the fields, moving the livestock from one field to another. There are so many visitors to the Peaks now that Alice and her father aren't able to move the animals at the weekend because the lanes are too crowded for them to get them about safely. But they're pleased to see so many tourists, especially as the overseas numbers increase and they're always happy to answer their questions about what they do, the animals, the land, and about life in the Peaks.

Alice seems positive about her life as a farmer, which is

good to hear – I know that there are many who feel that the public don't properly appreciate farmers. It will be interesting to see if she can make a go of it, with or without her sister.

It's time for me to crack on though. 'See you, Alice! Look after them sheep!' I call out.

I pass the seventeenth-century farmhouse, staying alongside the twisting and turning River Noe as I come to an old stone bridge. There are small copses of trees on either side of the river and track and beyond the fields, sheep drifting in lines up the hillsides. With the tempting sight of the moors looming ever larger, I'm getting closer to the end of the valley now and I can hear those big, beautiful hills calling to me.

The path is more like a small road now, deliberately, to help the farmers; it's even properly tarred. The National Trust owns lots of the farms around here and manages them to help conserve the sheep farming tradition and also to protect this beautiful landscape. There's a big ongoing programme, with plans not only to manage the moorland above, but also to provide a stable environment on these lowland fields which they'll have to use more intensively if they're to restrict the numbers of sheep allowed to graze on Kinder itself.

After centuries of farming, we're used to seeing the landscape as it looks to us today, but if we don't adapt to the changing conditions, we'll see a very different landscape. The peat of the Peak District is a valuable source of carbon storage – larger than the forests of England and France combined, but when the bogs become eroded by over-grazing, pollution, foot-fall or fire damage, they start leaking carbon dioxide instead of storing it. So, the area requires active forward-thinking land management. It's important to act now because the number of visitors is only going to go up – and we want to provide the farmers and other local people – artisans, shop and café owners – with a reasonable expectation of earning a living. It's a delicate balance that requires consultation and a level of investment. There's a big restoration programme going on up on these high moors, reseeding areas of exposed peat with heather and planting the pretty cotton grass.

It's only a short walk to my next stop. I'm approaching a string of picturesque old stone buildings that look like something out of *Wuthering Heights*. As I get closer I can hear the sounds of creativity reverberating from behind a stable door. Inside I find a genius woodman called – would you believe – Robin Wood.

Robin makes wooden bowls the old-fashioned way, on a 'foot-powered pole lathe'. The last craftsman in England who used this method died in 1958, so Robin really is a unique exponent of the craft. But he's also a man of his time. His craft might be a throwback to the past, but he's definitely not living there. Check out the Instagram video he posted of himself hewing a large piece of wood with an axe after a visit to the pub. He's decked out in his party shirt and banging away at the wood in time to the house music he loves. I like him immediately.

The first thing I have to know is if Robin changed his name when he started this job. Surely he can't have chosen to work with wood because he's called . . . Wood?

Robin laughs. 'No, no, I used to work for the National Trust,' he says.

Hmm – I bet he worked on the forestry side then.

Yep, turns out he did. I love this idea – people say, if the face fits . . . but what if the name does? Like Frances *Crook*, former Chief Executive of the Howard League for Penal Reform. Or an ex-MD of the Danone dairy group, Bruno *Fromage* or Bob *Flowerdew*, the gardener. I could go on.

It was when Robin visited the Museum for English Rural Life (MERL) in Reading, and stared into one of those dusty cabinets that I usually breeze past ('no – it's not a boring cabinet,' Robin declares, 'museums are great places'), looking for the more interesting stuff, that he caught sight of craftsman George Lailey's lathe and working tools. 'It was really exciting to me,' he says simply.

George Lailey was the last man working in Britain who made wooden bowls on a foot-powered lathe and, when he died, at the end of the 1950s, the craft died with him. Robin, however, on seeing George's tools, thought, why isn't anyone doing that? So, Robin began.

I thought I had the answer why – we stopped eating off wooden bowls years ago – but Robin tells me they were completely standard for centuries: 'Everyone ate from wooden bowls, from AD500 to the 1500s.' When the Tudor warship the *Mary Rose*, which sank in 1545, was salvaged in 1982, astonishing finds were made – including the discovery of pewter plates used by the officers and wooden bowls for the men. Ordinarily these plain, working men's items would have been thrown away so it was a rare find for the archaeologists. But tastes and industry changed and through the seventeenth and eighteenth centuries, the Stoke potteries kicked off and started to produce cheap industrial porcelain, which is still very much in use today.

For the past twenty years, Robin's been working full-time making wooden bowls this way, but is he the only one doing this?

'I've taught quite a lot of people, so I'm not the only one doing this now,' he says. 'I'm the only person who does it full-time. It was a completely extinct craft when I started and now there are a lot of people who can do it ... [T]here's people who've watched the videos I've uploaded to YouTube – people as far away as Japan, the States, Scandinavia. I love the mix of medieval craft and twenty-first-century media.'

Does he think his family will follow in his footsteps?

'I don't think my children will do this. My eldest daughter, who's twenty-one, is working with a clog maker, the last full-time clog maker in the country.' Mmm, still fairly niche, I think.

I wonder about the community– is Edale a good place to be if you're a wooden bowl maker? 'Edale's an amazing community, there's all sorts of people. We all mix – drystone wallers, theatre set designers, world-class rock stars – Jarvis Cocker lives in the village,' Robin comments.

Of course, I want to know how much one of his bowls would cost me – it's a pretty labour-intensive way to make a bowl and as each one is handcrafted, there's no mass production or anything like that. What if I were a passer-by, walking the Pennine Way, and I happened to come across Robin's workshop, I ask, would I be able to buy a bowl from him on the spot?

'I hardly sell anything from the door,' he says. 'I hardly have any finished bowls here. I sell nearly everything direct, over the internet, but I do sell through one outlet in Mayfair, called the New Craftsman, full of traditional crafts.'

The cost varies from style to style. The longer Robin has to spend at the lathe, the larger the piece of wood he's working from will all have an impact on price. 'My bowls are pretty distinctive. The one I'm making now is from a very special 162-year-old beech tree and the design is inspired by tenth-century Irish bowls. That'll be £65 – but it'll last fifty years.'

My eyes are drawn to a HUGE bowl in the corner of his workshop, over a metre in diameter. When I enquire about that, he says, '*That*, when it's finished (and they take a long time), will cost thousands.' Why do I always pick the expensive stuff? Never mind. It won't fit in my backpack anyway.

I do love what Robin does and how he effortlessly mixes the old with the new – making wooden bowls by hand and demonstrating the craft on YouTube to anyone who wants to learn how to do it. How he uses tools that a medieval craftsman would recognize, but spends his weekends at clubs in Sheffield, Manchester or Nottingham, dancing to techno and house music. I wonder how many other clubbers have come straight from a medieval workshop?

It turns out that we've met before – I presented him with an award from the Campaign to the Protect Rural England about ten years ago, in Sheffield (Robin also handmakes bridges, which is what the award was for; they're rather lovely, too).

Reluctantly I say goodbye; there's a lot still for me to do today, so it's time to move on. Robin hands me a small wooden bowl from his workshop.

'For you,' he smiles.

'Oh Mr Wood [I can't get over that name], thank you,' I say. 'I can't wait to have my breakfast from it.'

I head out past the buildings next to Robin's workshop and through the gateway. The river, still trundling alongside the track here, is lively as it noisily tumbles down from the hills above. Robin says I might see the source when I'm up there. The cosiness of the valley starts to fade away as I get closer to the open slopes of the hills ahead and, apart from the little plantation of trees that the National Trust has started as part of its management of the land, the only growth around me is the knee-high grasses on the edges of the track.

I'm momentarily distracted by the clatter of horses' hooves.

A couple of riders come up behind me, the two ladies chatting away as they ride along next to each other.

'Afternoon ladies,' I call. 'This is a very good walking trail – what happens when you get higher up the valley with the horses?'

'Well, you can actually join the Trans-Pennine Trail, which is a long-distance riding route. From here it's a four-hour ride, all off-road, so it's fantastic – provided the weather's good,' one of the riders, Alison Payne, says. She's an abdominal surgeon and riding is her 'antidote to the stresses of the NHS' – which bears out the message on the bench I sat by with my dad earlier. Alison came to Sheffield as a student and never left the area, moving to Edale to 'live the dream' in the country. I know all about this, as I grew up in Sheffield, I tell her.

'It's an addiction that comes back to bite you,' she agrees. Her friend Bobbie is a welcome riding companion and they get out here as often as they can The views must be even better from on top of a horse, I think.

Alison's riding a native Pennine pony, which in previous centuries would have been carrying lead from the mines on the jaggers' trails. The jaggers (derived from the old English word 'jag' meaning 'a load') were often farmers who did this work to get extra income. Packhorses were used to transport goods and materials before the transport revolutions of the canals, followed by the railways, both of which transformed Britain's trade routes.

Alison prepares me for the steep climb up ahead, Jacob's Ladder. This, as I've mentioned before, is the tough climb of the walk. In fact it's a tough climb of *any* walk.

'The less steep way is to go up the old packhorse trail on the zigzags,' she says helpfully, 'but it does take longer.'

'I'm not going to cheat,' I reply. 'How long will it take me?'

'Oh,' she says. 'It depends on how many times you have to stop and admire the view.'

And what a view it is, even from here. A little further up this wide pathway I can make out a pretty stone packhorse bridge that I'm going to have to walk across to get to the first of the giant flagstones that make up Jacob's Ladder which winds its way up through the deep folding cloughs.

Apparently Jacob Marshall (the 'Jacob' of the 'Ladder') was a canny Edale farmer a few centuries back, who got fed up with following his pony winding in a slow zigzag up the steep hill and decided to build the steps for a quicker route up so that he'd then have a lovely rest until the ponies turned up. He was probably one of the earliest fell runners who liked the fast way up . . . a man after my own heart! Nice one Jacob! So, let's get up there . . . and thanks for the leg up.

It's all about the incline on a stretch like Jacob's Ladder. As long as you're fit enough to tackle the incline, you're okay. The ladies and their horses have gone on ahead as they're a bit faster than me. As Alison's horse, Charley, trots off, he lets out a huge fart. We all let out ripples of childish giggles and I say to Colin, the soundman, 'I hope you got that, Col. Perfect timing. We can use it for the opening credits.'

Kinder Scout is still a long way off. One of the deceptive things about walking here is that what you think of as the top of the moors, when you're down in the valley, is not the top. It's just the first of a series of plateaus and this is just one of the many things that defeats a lot of walkers – they clamber up the steep sides of the Peaks and reach what they think is a good high point to take stock of where they are and look about them, but then realize that they're still quite some way below being able to do that. And, when the weather closes in, walking here can become quite tricky, indeed.

But what if you live here all the time? We hear a lot about the problems of the countryside, and of course they're real – the dwindling numbers of jobs, the problems farmers face, the squeeze on affordable housing – and yet, there are people everywhere looking to find a better way of life outside of the big towns and cities. I've met many of them today already: Robin who escaped to his wood shed; Alison's a top surgeon yet rooted in this place; and the little village of Edale has been adopted by a sensitive rock star like Jarvis Cocker. It goes to show that the countryside is always adapting and evolving, just so long as there are always people happy to work hard to keep it going.

The valley has closed in now and the hills are also pressing in on me. It's exciting to feel I'm now at the start of the moors proper. The hillsides are bare and I'm enjoying the crunch of my boots on the trail as I approach the tiny stone bridge in front of me and apart from the water, there are very few other sounds now the horses have moved on.

At last, I reach the foot of Jacob's Ladder. It's a marvellous higgledy-piggledy path and I can see how worn some of the stones are. In the days of the packhorses, the ponies would be led up the zigzag route while the men walked up the quicker, but steeper path here, allowing them time for that all important breather at the top. The Ladder starts right after the pretty stone bridge that spans just over 3.5m (12ft) and is narrow enough to allow only one packhorse at a time (I forgot to bring mine with me, damn), before the path snakes up the grassy slopes that rise in slow waves, cutting through the steep valley to the top and the moor.

These steps are really the only big challenge of this walk and the secret it is to take them at your own pace. Remember, the hills will still be waiting for you, however slowly you get up to them. Anyone, though, can get tired out and if you're finding the going tough, then I like to recall what that great Alfred Wainwright used to say: 'Just put one foot in front of the other and you can't go wrong.' It's a tiring challenge, but I know I'll recover quickly once we reach the top here; it's just about having the determination to keep going. As it turns out, I'm a mountain goat type and I quite like hopping from rock to rock. Eventually, I reach the top of the Ladder and I can finally turn and look back out over the valley where I've come from and take in the view.

It is picture perfect. If only I had a camera with me. (Oh, I do. A big one.) Sometimes, you just can't put into words anything substantial enough to match the reality. I can only say this is *exactly* what I picture when someone says 'the English countryside': a collection of little houses and trees nestled into a deep green valley, lush slopes folding into one another – palettes of olive, khaki, avocado, emerald and yellow converge. Next to me is the River Noe, but a different one to that found down in the valley, where it was a lovely babbling stream, shadowing the path all the way from Upper Booth, where I met Alice, what seems like only a few moments ago. Up here, it's an angry little race, shooting off the rocks. Little side streams join it, pouring out of the hillside and, as I get higher and higher, the stream becomes no less ferocious, just smaller.

In the distance ahead are some bumpy small boulders – near there is my target and, while the stones doesn't look like much, I know when I get to them, they'll be enormous and I intend to climb up on to them and beat my fists on my chest like something out of *Planet of The Apes*, calling out over the valley. As I finally reach the top of Jacob's Ladder, I should be on fire, but a bitter wind has whipped up and a mist is circling all around me. It's come from nowhere. I pull on a hat and close up my jacket and get my bearings. As expected, what looked like a peak from down below is now revealed as a sprawling plateau with rocky outcrops scattered here and there. I've another stretch to climb in order to get to the trig point that marks Kinder Scout and the entire landscape has started to change; it's now boggy and damp underfoot as I walk on. As I reach Kinder Low, I'm reminded again how wild and exposed these moorlands are.

The mist and fog settle around the Peaks and catch unsuspecting walkers by surprise all the time. That's why all the leaflets and guides tell walkers to carry a compass and know how to read a map (I just bring a television crew along with me so we can all get lost together). What might seem like a straightforward hike from a pub can swiftly turn into a problem if you're not prepared for this as the Mountain Rescue team knows well. Last year, it took part in 140 incidents on this stretch of the moors alone – I know this because I'm about to interrupt one of their training exercises and meet some of the volunteers who make up those teams.

It's amazing that such an essential service is peopled by volunteers here. In places like Switzerland, you have to have insurance to make use of the rescue services or pay the thousands and thousands of Euros it costs to be taken or airlifted off a mountain. In Britain, they're all volunteers who give up their time FOR FREE. So, if you take a tumble, twist your ankle or get lost, these incredibly noble men, women and dogs will come and do their very best to find, rescue and save you. We take our rescue men and women for granted in this country, and I'd say that probably most people don't realize these people don't get paid.

This particular group, the Kinder Mountain rescue team, was started in 1971. It's made up of a team of about fifty volunteers and, in any given week, they can be called on to deal with such varied problems as cases of exposure, exhaustion, injury or missing persons. They'll be helping walkers, mountain bikers and providing assistance to the air ambulance, medical teams and police, who are all also involved in rescues.

Today though is dog-training day. The team's put a 'body' out on the moor in the mist that has suddenly risen about us and they let the dog hunt for her. When the hound finds the victim she stays by the body and barks to let her handlers know where to come to. Today's body is a bit different . . . I have some lovely fans and friends and one of them took part in a charity auction raising money for St Luke's, a Sheffield-based hospice of which I'm patron, which offers free care and support for adults of all ages with life-limiting illnesses. (The hospice network in this country, like the volunteer one, is another phenomenal resource.) Debbie, a kind-hearted, glamorous northern woman, who I've met at several charity events, raised her hand and paid a substantial sum of money to come and spend a 'day on location filming with Julia and her crew'. What she didn't expect is for us to throw her in a ditch at the top of the moor. As the exercise begins, I ask Debbie, who's lying flat out in the deep heather, how she's doing.

'Are you okay, chuck?'

'Absolutely fine, Julia. I can stay here as long as you want.'

'Are you cold?'

'Nope, got the tweeds on, warm as toast,' comes her prosaic response.

I love northerners – there's no poncing around. Luckily, Flash, the hero pooch, is on top form and sniffs her out in no time at all, barking wildly. Perfect. Job well done. It's incredible to watch these dogs and their handlers at work. I'd be very grateful to see Flash's nose coming towards me if I were stranded in a trench. But now, it's time for a big flask of tea.

I say my goodbyes after a nice warming brew and leave the guys to their training. I keep heading out across the upper moorland – I'm off the Pennine Way trail now and skirting eastwards across a completely different landscape. It feels similar to parts of volcanic Iceland that I've hiked across. The peat bog is a dark brown, almost black and you can clearly see the erosion channels that all the walkers have caused. Craggy rock formations are dotted everywhere and add to the lunar atmosphere. They're like giant Henry Moore sculptures, buried deep into the earth, carved by ice, wind and water over the centuries. Boulderers, rock climbers and scramblers love it up here. There are so many rugged rocky beauties to get stuck into or onto.

I'm looking for the trig point that marks Kinder Scout proper. It can be tricky to find your way here in mist or low rain, the route isn't easy to follow, people have been known to walk just 20m (65 feet) past the trig and miss it. That doesn't sound bad but as the trig marks the start of the Pennine Way, if you are metres off here, you're going to be walking across an awful lot of moor later on (Kinder Scout alone is over 1,700 acres) trying to find your way back on to the proper route. Which is why the volunteer rescue team are so important and why they get so many call outs.

For me, this is the most exciting part of the walk. In all my years of hiking all over the world and all over the country, I've never been to the 'birthplace of walking', Kinder Scout. My dad always calls it the 'spiritual' birthplace of walking. Despite the detailed 1 in 25,000 scale map and great guidance from the mountain team, it's not that easy to find and it's, therefore, easy to see why so many people get lost up here in bad weather

Kinder Scout's significance to walking in Britain is down to the efforts of a remarkable group of brave people. Kinder Scout is the scene of a mass trespass that took place in April 1932. Across this moor, about 400 ordinary walkers from Manchester and Sheffield, led by twenty-year-old Benny Rothman, scuffled with gamekeepers and police in a protest against limited access to the countryside. In a stand-off with landowners, who wanted to keep this land private for grouse shooting, Rothman and four other walkers were arrested and jailed for periods of between three and six months – trespass wasn't a criminal offence but they were convicted of violence against the gamekeepers. The national outrage was so great that the walkers were released. That one day of mass protest right here released the floodgates over the next decades to open up land to the walking public, leading to the creation of our first ever national park, right here, in 1951, called the Peak District National Park.

According to my dad: 'If you lived in the country, you walked anyway, but what they did gave urban Britain the right to walk freely. Anywhere. The majority of Britons didn't have that right – and now they do.'

It's hard to imagine a time when it was ever difficult or dangerous to go walking and explore our countryside, but many people were locked out of places like this. Gamekeepers blocked their way. That 'right to roam' protest, all those years ago, and the thirst for access it represented, is why Britain has so many public footpaths today. When people like Alfred Wainwright, and many others, including organizations like the Ramblers' Association, introduced the general public to the glories of the countryside, they probably didn't anticipate quite how many would step out every weekend to walk the trails and paths and show that our right to roam remains a precious and deeply appreciated gift.

Despite the erosion up on the plateau, this organic earthy landscape is wildly attractive. I walk through a tunnel of deep crevices in the wet blanket bog twice my height. On the high edges above me I can make out fringes of reseeded cotton grass and heather. I step out of the maze into an open area where I can't see a speck of green: just black earth and dark boulders strewn everywhere, with gritty sand underfoot. I feel as if I'm walking on an abandoned seabed: it's as if the water and all other life forms have been sucked away by some strange force. And then I see something that I've been waiting my entire walking life to see – the trig point for Kinder Scout, known (confusingly) as Kinder Low. This is the very spot where Benny and his gang took on the landed gentry for their right to enjoy our green bits. As if they should have had to fight for it.

The trig point is on a rock which I clamber to the top of. I'm now at the official high point, 636 m (2,087 ft) above sea level. I lean forward to kiss the ugly bit of white triangular concrete. I've kissed worse. 'The mecca of walking,' I declare to the camera. I'm feeling quite emotional.

I'm lucky that lots of my 'never forget' moments have been captured on film: my flight in a Red Arrow, my microlight over Victoria Falls, my up-close encounters with a grey whale and black bears, my first ascent of Scafell and now my first moment on Kinder. This though I really never will forget. I scan the amazing views – out to the west to Hayfield, Whalley Range and Manchester and to the east, Sheffield, my school town.

As I walk back towards the crew I notice a new very tall addition to the crew whispering excitedly in Eric the director's ear. 'Is that J-J-Julia Bradbury?' 'It's me!' I smile, reaching out my hand. 'This is one of the happiest days of my life,' claims the tall stranger, grabbing my paw. 'I'm only up here for a quick walk . . . I never thought . . . you . . .'

David Cooper, a keen walker as you've worked out, asked me not to forget his name because he would be in touch. True to his word, a few weeks later a photo arrived for me to sign with a lovely letter about how touched he had been to meet me that day. Me too Dave, it made my Kinder Scout moment even more memorable.

Although this may feel like the end of the walk, there's still a strange little circle back to do in order for us to reach our planned destination, the crazy rock formation known as Noe Stool. We're actually higher than Noe Stool here, but I can't see it from the trig point, because it's so broad that you get a false horizon (much like an infinity pool . . . and it's almost as wet as a pool here today). For the first time, my boots are thick with peaty cloggy mud and it's a bit like walking through treacle pudding. I can't imagine running in it but that's what Damian Hall is doing, right towards me. Damian wrote the official guidebook to the Pennine Way, but that's not why we're catching up today. He also managed to complete the absolutely bonkers long-distance fell run known as The Spine, which covers the entire Pennine Way route in the height of winter – in about a week. Damian, I say, that's about 61km (38 miles) per day – that's one-and-a-half marathons, every day, for a week. In the snow and biting wind.

'Yes,' he agrees. 'It took me seven weeks to recover. But the winner that year came in at about four-and-a-half days.'

Four-and-a-half days to run all that distance? No thanks. Well, it has to be asked – why'd *you* do it? I say.

'A kind of madness – or mid-life crisis – it's about having great adventures outdoors. I'd walked it so many times for writing the Pennine Way guidebook. I love running so it was the ultimate challenge for me! It's good fun.'

'It's good fun? Good fun?' I parrot. 'You're lying. But will you go again?'

He laughs. 'No, I don't think so. My tendons and my wife won't let me, not with a one-year-old boy and four-year-old girl at home.'

'We've nearly done the first five miles today,' I tell Damian. 'So tell me, what's the rest of it like?'

'It's just the ultimate, longest, hardest, toughest trail for walking in England – it follows the backbone of the Pennines. From here, going north through Derbyshire, Yorkshire, Cumbria, Northumberland and into Scotland – it's the Big One. You skirt big cities, but it feels very remote,' states Damien. 'The creator of this National Trail, the oldest there is, Tom Stephenson, began it right here in honour of the Mass Trespass of 1932 – that struggle.'

I mention that Alfred Wainwright wasn't such a fan . . .

'Alfred was caught by some bad weather when he attempted the walk and that must have put him off,' Damian says kindly.

'Well, thanks Damian,' I say. 'You'd better get on with your running now, you crazy man!' As I push off through the cloggyness towards my end goal, I mutter, 'Does anyone have any ski poles?'

I'm getting close to Noe Stool, which looked a lot smaller from further away. I turn around to glance at this weirdly beautiful place one more time. The windswept upland gritstone plateau is quite unique, I think to myself.

There are tons of unusual, beautiful-looking rocks up here, but Noe Stool is particularly distinctive: it's the only anvil-shaped one. This rock is perched on the edge, looking down over the rolling hillsides below. The temptation to climb on top of it and become part of the skyline has been too great for hundreds, probably, thousands of people, so I'm not going to be left out. I find a foothold on the side of the huge boulder and reach up to clasp onto a corner of the rock. After a couple of moves I'm on the top, and here is my treat: to stand high, looking out at a final view of the Vale of Edale. An all-encompassing picture of tranquillity.

There's a great contrast between the almost domestic serenity of the valley floor, the seemingly peaceful nature of life there, with little fields edged by walls and broad-leafed trees, contrasted to the rugged headland up here, where the fields give way to wide open spaces. The ridge of the Peaks marks the boundary between land and sky, etching out the very limits of their power, almost as if someone has drawn it there: it couldn't be more perfect.

Someone has chosen to heighten the experience by peppering

the fields far down below with little fluffy white dots, the flocks of sheep under the control of shepherdesses like Alice.

For me, this walk has a big place in my heart. It's full of childhood memories, but for millions of other walkers coming here, it is a tribute to those who challenged the status quo in order that they, their children, their descendants and all the rest of us might have the chance to experience this beauty first-hand, whenever we choose to. It's a salute to the movement that ignited the 'freedom to roam' torch.

Somewhere down there, in another time, my dad was born; he took my mum on their honeymoon in one of those little villages; and he brought me to so many of the surrounding upland moors and craggy rock faces up here, although not this one. And more than anything, I wish dad were here with me now. I wish I could hold his hand just like I did when I was a little girl, exhausted but thrilled to be with him, having completed this, 'our Everest', together.

WALKER'S GUIDE:
WHERE TO STAY, WHERE TO EAT,
WHAT TO SEE, WHAT TO DO

To finish: The Nags Head in Edale (Hope Valley, Derbyshire S33 7ZD) was the perfect place for a pint with my dad: and what higher praise can you give a pub?

To eat: Stonecroft Cottage (Edale S33 7ZA – https://curatedby. theoutdoorguide.co.uk/stonecroft) does a specialist gluten-free menu, and is also an excellent place to stay . . .

To stay: . . . as are Underleigh House and Losehill Hotel (both Losehill Lane, Edale Road S33 6AF).

To see: Kinder Scout: no less than the birthplace of walking in this country: there's literally no more appropriate place for a walker to visit (http://www.peakdistrictinformation.com/features/kinder.php).